EGYPTIAN ART

EGYPTIAN ART

IN THE EGYPTIAN MUSEUM
OF TURIN

PAINTINGS · SCULPTURE · FURNITURE

TEXTILES · CERAMICS · PAPYRI

Ernesto Scamuzzi

HARRY N. ABRAMS, INC., *Publishers*

NEW YORK

Translated by Barbara Arnett Melchiori

Library of Congress Catalog Card Number: 65-13910
Harry N. Abrams, Incorporated, New York

Printed and bound in Japan

LIST OF PLATES

PREFACE

There is no evidence that Turin possessed an important collection of Egyptian antiquities until the eighteenth century: the few monuments known to have existed in the city before this date, according to a tradition which is still current today although there is no positive evidence for this, had changed hands in 1630, passing to the dukes of the house of Savoy from the house of Gonzaga in Mantua. The most noteworthy are the Table of Isis (also known as the Table of Cardinal Bembo) (1), and a stone bust of a woman which was erroneously believed to be antique, or rather Egyptian, on account of some signs in an unknown language visible here and there on the breast and face; in the years 1761-62 these gave rise to discussion between Turbeville Needham, an Englishman, and the Italian antiquarian G. Bartoli.

The three imposing stone statues now exhibited in the Sculpture Rooms on the ground floor were brought to the city by a Paduan naturalist, Vitaliano Donati (1717-62), who held the chair of Natural History and Botany in the University of Turin. Donati also imported a collection of some three hundred less important objects (Greek, Roman and Coptic lamps; animal mummies, amulets, etc.) which he had collected in the course of his research and explorations in Egypt and the Near East, carried out under the auspices of King Charles Emmanuel III. The first of these statues, in red granite, reproduces an unidentified ruler living at the time of the so-called Second Intermediate Period; Ramesses II of the 19th dynasty later attributed this statue to himself (see Plate LXII). The second, in black granite, represents the lion-headed goddess Sachmis, seated on a throne along the sides of which the name of King Amenhotep III of the 18th dynasty is legible. The third, also in black granite, considerably mutilated and damaged, represents a goddess who has never been conclusively identified, the work of a skilled artist of the 18th dynasty (Plate XXXIV).

In 1824 Turin received the richest collection of Egyptian antiquities either in Italy or abroad, when King Charles Felix (1821-31) signed the act of purchase of the first and

(1) Displayed in Exhibition Room IV, on the first floor.

most famous collection of Egyptian monuments and documents, following a long period of negotiations initiated by his brother and predecessor, Victor Emmanuel I. This collection had been assembled with praiseworthy industry and acumen by Bernardino Drovetti (1776-1852) of Barbania, in the Canavese district of Piedmont, during the years he spent in Egypt as French consul general and as the wise and influential counsellor of the viceroy of Egypt, Mohammed Ali, and his son Ibrahim Pasha (1).

Many factors contributed to the fortunate outcome of the negotiations: on the one hand, Drovetti's love for his native land and his determination that his beloved collection should remain in Italy; on the other, the presence and intervention of such eminent men as Count Prospero Balbo, Count Carlo Vidua di Conzano and Cavaliere Cesare Saluzzo.

By the desire of Charles Felix, the Drovetti collection was housed and arranged for exhibition in rooms of the palace which still goes by the name of the Palazzo dell'Accademia delle Scienze (2), one of the most imposing and monumental buildings in the city. Built in 1678 on land donated by the second Queen Mother, Maria Giovanna Battista di Nemours, wife of Charles Emmanuel II, it was designed by a famous Modenese architect, Father Guarino Guarini, as a stately college for the nobility who wished to become churchmen under the teaching of the Jesuit Order.

To celebrate the purchase of the Drovetti collection Charles Felix embellished the main entrance of the Palace, on what is now known as Via Accademia delle Scienze, by adding an

(1) It is interesting to note, on several of the statues of kings or gods which form part of the collection, French inscriptions engraved by Jean-Jacques Rifaud (1786-1845) of Marseilles, which are full of unsuspected but entertaining mistakes. Rifaud *au service de M. Drovetti* assisted him in the discovery of precious statues in the territory of ancient Thebes, in 1818, and wrote a number of travel books detailing his adventures in Egypt and Nubia.

The statues reproduced in the present volume which bear inscriptions by Rifaud are those of Tuthmosis I (Plate XXII), of Tuthmosis III (Plate XXIV), of the sphinx of Amenhotep III (Plate XXVIII), the group of Amon-Ra and Tut-ankh-amon (Plate XXX), of the god Ptah (Plate XXXIII) which is reproduced above as an example, of Ramesses II (Plate LVII), of Ramesses II between Amon-Ra and Mut (Plate LX), and of the goddess Sachmis (Plate LXXXVI).

(2) The Accademia delle Scienze, founded by Count Giuseppe Angelo Saluzzo di Monesiglio, the physician G. Cigna, and the mathematician G. L. Lagrange, has occupied part of the palace since 1783.

Wooden bust of Bernardino Drovetti

ornamental marble balcony supported by four tall monolithic pillars, designed by Talucchi; this is recorded in the Latin epigraph engraved along its base:

REX CAROLUS FELIX MUSEO MONUMENTIS AEGYPTIIS ADAUCTO MDCCCXXIV

The honour of being the first visitor to the Drovetti collection in 1824, the year of its opening, was reserved, and rightly, for Jean-François Champollion, the French scholar celebrated for deciphering Egyptian texts. He examined at leisure the art treasures and documents, and carried away such a pleasant impression of his stay, and of the cordial welcome he met with at the hands of the Turinese with whom he was soon on terms of friendship, that the following year he returned to Turin. The impression left on him by his study of the antiquities in the Drovetti collection can be measured by the heartfelt and enthusiastic appreciation in his two *Lettres relatives au Musée Royale Égyptien de Turin* addressed to the Duke de Blacas d'Aulps, "premier Gentilhomme de Chambre," etc. (1), in August and December 1824.

Among the many statues in the Drovetti collection, the black granite figure of Ramesses II (Plate LVII) which stands against the wall facing the entrance of Sculpture Room I was especially admired by Champollion: in recollection of this preference, when news of the death of the decipherer reached Turin in 1832, the "moderatores rei litterariae" placed above the statue a tablet bearing the following Latin inscription:

HONORI ET MEMORIAE
IOANNIS FRANCISCI CHAMPOLLIONIS
QUI ARCANAE AEGYPTIORUM SCRIPTURAE
RECONDITAM DOCTRINAM PRIMUS APERUIT
MONUMENTA AEGYPTIA
REGIS VICTORII EMMANUELIS LIBERALITATE CONQUISITA
IN HIS AEDIBUS DOCTE INVISIT SCRIPTIS INLUSTRAVIT
MODERATORES REI LITTERARIAE
STATIM AC DE MORTE CELEBERRIMI VIRI NUNTIATUM EST
MENSE MARTIO ANNO MDCCCXXXII
PRINCIPATUS REGIS CAROLI ALBERTI SECUNDO (2)

The few Egyptian antiquities already existing in the city were soon annexed to the nucleus of the outstanding Drovetti collection, to which, in the course of the nineteenth century, gifts were added from private donors (particular mention should be made of Cava-

(1) Both letters were printed in Paris, and dated 1824 and 1826.
(2) The statement that the Drovetti collection was purchased through the good offices of Victor Emmanuel I, whose voluntary abdication took place in 1821, is not accurate. The reader will notice the omission—far from casual—of all mention of Victor Emmanuel's brother and successor, Charles Felix.

liere Busca, Santoni, H.-W. Seton-Karr, Victor Emmanuel II, and Cavaliere Zucchi); antiquities were also obtained through the purchase of minor collections (such as that of Giuseppe Sossio, in 1833), exchanges with other Italian museums, and purchases made in Egypt by Ernesto Schiaparelli at the end of the century. In the early twentieth century, the already noteworthy importance of the Museum was increased by the findings in Egypt of the many expeditions to famous historical sites, organized between 1903 and 1920 by Ernesto Schiaparelli. These, from north to south, comprised Heliopolis, Giza, Hermopolis Megale, Assiut, Hammamia, Qau el Kebir, Bibân el-Harīm (Valley of the Queens), Bibân el-Molûk (Valley of the Kings), Der el-Medîna, Gebelein, Aswan. In 1930 and 1937 Giulio Farina, who in 1928 succeeded Schiaparelli as director of the Museum, carried out fruitful excavations in the predynastic necropolises of Assiut and Gebelein. Farina's name will always be remembered in connection with the discovery of priceless fragments, unique at the present state of our knowledge, of the earliest Egyptian painting on linen cloth (Plates I-V).

At present the antiquities in the possession of the Museum are on show in the Sculpture Rooms on the ground floor and in the Exhibition Rooms on the first floor. The Sculpture Rooms consist of two large rectangular halls adjacent to one another, the walls of which are lined with statues of kings, private citizens and gods, from the Old Kingdom to the era of the Ptolemies. On the left-hand wall of Sculpture Room I stands a valued wooden bust of Drovetti, below which is the memorial inscription composed by Luigi Cibrario:

A MEMORIA ED ONORE
DI BERNARDINO DROVETTI
DA BARBANIA
CHE CONSOLE GENERALE DI FRANCIA IN EGITTO
ADUNO' IN LUNGHI ANNI DI SAPIENTI RICERCHE
QUESTE ANTICHITA' EGIZIANE
PROCURANDO POI CHE DIVENTASSERO
ACQUISTO DEI NOSTRI PRINCIPI
ED UNA FRA LE GLORIE PIEMONTESI (1)

Today the art treasures in the rooms on the first floor are no longer exhibited in the old-fashioned arrangement of the nineteenth century, by which sculptures and documents were placed in certain corners or against certain walls according to the space available or the

(1) " To the memory and in honour of Bernardino Drovetti of Barbania who as French Consul General in Egypt collected these Egyptian antiquities in the course of long years of patient research, and enabled them to be purchased by our Princes and to become one of the glories of Piedmont. "

effect which the custodian of the time wished to achieve. An oil painting on cardboard, dated July 16, 1881 and signed Lorenzo Delleani (1840-1907), gives an idea of that effect. The old arrangement remained substantially unchanged until 1940, when the author of the present volume was enabled, soon after the end of the Second World War, to re-order the rooms with the intent of reorganizing a nineteenth-century Egyptian museum to present visitors with an up-to-date museum of Egyptian civilization. In the galleries, deliberately severe in style and fostering silent meditation and tranquil individual study, the exhibits follow one another in chronological order and according to type, but arranged at the same time to assist the visitor in acquiring a knowledge of the aspects of Egyptian civilization throughout history, from paleolithic to recorded history and Egypt's later decadence under the domination of the Greeks and then the Romans: the religious beliefs, the funeral cult, daily life and cultural activities, etc. The collection of no less than nineteen tempera wallpaintings, detached from the tomb of a high State official under the 11th dynasty, in Gebelein, alone constitutes a rarity, the largest collection of ancient Egyptian painting to be found in Italy.

The Egyptian Museum, the Automobile Museum and the Cinema Museum are undeniably the three most typical museums in Turin, but the Egyptian takes precedence, both in the city and elsewhere, as the best known, the Turin Museum *par excellence*. Its rooms have been and will continue to be traversed by ever-growing numbers of visitors from Turin, from Italy, and the rest of the world.

The present volume has been designed to serve a dual purpose: for those who have not visited the Museum, it should provide a knowledge of the importance and range of the collection by the selection and reproduction of sculptures and documents dating from the early predynastic period down to the Coptic era; for those others who visit the Museum at frequent intervals, it offers a selection of those antiquities which have particularly excited their curiosity or interest, and which they recall with admiration.

ERNESTO SCAMUZZI

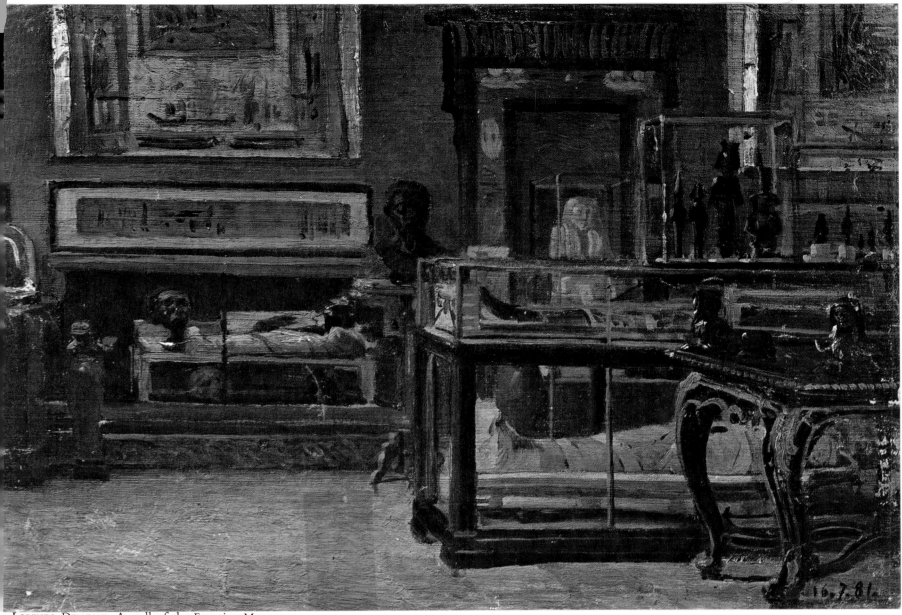

LORENZO DELLEANI, A wall of the Egyptian Museum.

Oil on cardboard. Dated 16.7.1881. Height 1 ft. 2¾ in., width 1 ft. 7¼ in.

Along the first half of the wall, from left to right, is an illustrated papyrus in a rectangular frame of black wood, with some mummies and mummy heads below, and the wooden bust of Drovetti. Toward the right is the wooden door-frame with architrave (the colouring of which was restored in Turin in the nineteenth century) removed from the tomb of the Vizier Neferrònpe and of Neferhotep, director of works in the Theban necropolis (in the district of the modern Der el-Medîna). This doorway can be seen today in the centre of the end wall of the First Exhibition Room on the first floor. The painting shows also the upper portion of the lid of a limestone sarcophagus now exhibited in Sculpture Room II; statuettes of the gods Osiris and Bes, and smaller statues of other deities. At a distance from the wall, on top of the black wooden frame, is a sarcophagus lid, and below is the sarcophagus containing a swathed mummy, now exhibited in Exhibition Room II on the first floor. Other objects are set out on a table, of which one end and two legs are shown in the picture.

Hanging on the wall are to be seen the lower portions of two modern paintings dealing with aspects of Egyptian life. These are typical of the many then displayed on the walls of the Museum, in keeping with the taste of the period; some were retained well into the present century.

PREDYNASTIC PERIOD

FOREWORD TO PLATES I–V

*In the course of the excavations carried out by the Italian Egyptological Expedition in 1930, **under the** **direction** of Giulio Farina, numerous portions of linen cloth were discovered in a tomb unearthed in a necropolis described by Farina as " prehistoric," in the region of Gebelein (Southern Egypt). In spite of a number of missing portions, these fragments were part of " a long canvas painted tapestry-wise." Farina provided no information regarding the type of tomb, the funeral equipment it contained or the way in which the body was buried. He wrote that the " long canvas " was discovered folded at the side of a mummy and that the damage suffered by the linen cloth was due to damp (cf. the fortnightly periodical " Sapere," 15th May 1939, p. 346).*

The differences in colouring of the " canvas " (roughly half is dark brown and the remainder a greyish ivory with ash-coloured markings) might be attributed to the different degrees in which parts of the cloth came into contact with the earth and the body. Nevertheless, bearing in mind the great disparity in the treatment of the human figure in the scenes which embellish both halves of the " canvas," which induces us to admit that there must have been not one but two painters of the scenes portrayed on the surviving portions, I believe that the hypothesis that two canvases were placed beside the mummy is worthy of acceptance. I shall return to this question later.

The portions recovered, after Erminia Caudana of the Turin Superintendency of Egyptian Antiquities had spent several months on their restoration, are now on display in wooden frames, protected by large sheets of glass, in the first half of Exhibition Room III on the first floor.

The fragments of linen cloth of what I shall call " canvas no. 1," which are distinguished by their dark brown colour, are all collected in the first frame. The following scenes are preserved:

Men and women in a funeral dance (Plate I)
Men and women among trees (Plate II)
The deceased hunting a hippopotamus (Plate III)
The deceased fishing (Plate IV)
Ships on a small scale, with many oars

The surviving fragments of " canvas no. 2," of lighter coloured cloth, displayed in the second frame, show two large ships with cabins, rowed by oars and steered by helmsmen.

Few colours are used: black, red, and white, the latter only for certain details on " canvas no. 1." These colours are the same as those on the predynastic wall paintings of Hierakonpolis, and outside Egypt are those found in use in Mesopotamia, always in very early times.

Colour was used by both painters as a means of figuration. The bodies of both men and women in " canvas no. 1 " are portrayed uniformly in red, without any distinction in colour as to sex. The female figure can be identified by a very long skirt worn from the waist down to the ground so as to hide the feet, and by the fullness of the hips. In general the female figure is shown as taller $(6\,^1/_4$ in.$)$ than the male, who is at most $3\,^1/_2$ in. The males wear no garments except white loin-cloths, knotted over one hip.

The painter of " canvas no. 1 " began by painting in red the triangular torsos of his figures, to which he added black blobs representing the heads. Also the black skirts were added later. The small ships, of which two are better preserved and the third is only a fragment, were depicted in red, then the oars were added in black, and lastly the oar-blades in red. Trees and plants are portrayed uniformly in black.

In respect of " canvas no. 2: " the two large ships were depicted in black with the cabins in red and black; the heads and busts of the oarsmen, the long oars and the helms were all in red. Farina found also a precious fragment of fringe belonging to this canvas, which is displayed in the bottom left-hand corner, measuring $4\,^1/_8$ in. $\times$ $2\,^1/_2$ in. (see Plate V).

As in the wall paintings of Hierakonpolis and in the scenes decorating pottery vases of the same period, there is no indication, even purely conventional, of the ground on which the figures stand and move, or of the water on which the ships should float.

I have put forward the hypothesis that there must have been two painters of these portions of linen cloth. The signature, so to speak, of both can be traced in their different treatment of the faces of the figures portrayed in the " canvases." The first, the painter of the figures on " canvas no. 1, " represents the head or the face of his figures, both male and female, with a black blob, giving no hint as to hair or head-dress. Entirely devoid of descriptive detail, the black blobs represent now the head, now the face, and this whether full-face or profile.

The painter of the figures in " canvas no. 2, " all of which are male, is clearly distinguishable from the first in that, having eliminated the conventional black blob, he tries to reproduce the faces in his scene in right profile and to mark certain details, yet so roughly that it is uncertain whether the protuberances visible on the faces are to be taken for the noses or the beards of the oarsmen.

The way in which the scenes on the fragments of " canvas no. 1 " are displayed for visitors aims at furnishing an interpretation. It is impossible to set them out and arrange them in accordance with the original scheme of the ancient painter. Each of the fragments may have been in an entirely different position, higher or lower, further to the left or the right.

The present arrangement, which enables the visitor to examine them in detail, is as follows:

a) *above*	Men and women in a funeral dance	Men and women among trees	
b) *below*	The deceased hunting a hippopotamus	The deceased fishing	Small scale ships, with many oars

The two predynastic " canvases " can be attributed to the first phase of the so-called Nagadah civilization, beginning from the first half of the 4th millennium B.C.

PLATE I

MEN AND WOMEN IN A FUNERAL DANCE

Scene assembled from eight fragments of linen cloth. Height of the whole scene in its present arrangement 10 ¹/₂ in., width 1 ft. 9 in. From the excavations of Giulio Farina in the necropolis of Gebelein, 1930

The clue followed for the arrangement of the scene of the funeral dance was given by the first fragment on the left, which shows a large female figure with small male figures beside and below: it seemed fitting to close the scene on the right with a similar female figure, in the same posture and of the same dimensions as the former.

The space between the two women is occupied by male figures arranged in three parallel rows: those on the first row, beginning from the top, are wearing white loin-cloths, as we can see from the remnants around the waist of the first figure from the left, and have both arms raised; those on the second row have only one arm raised, while those on the third stand hand in hand with their arms down.

It is impossible to ascertain the number of figures originally present in each row. The third or bottom row suggests that the top row may likewise originally have continued beyond the limits marked by the two large female figures.

PLATE II

MEN AND WOMEN AMONG TREES

*Scene assembled from fragments. Height of present arrangement 1 ft. 1 ³/₈ in., width about 1 ft. 4 ¹/₂ in.
From the excavations of Giulio Farina in the necropolis of Gebelein, 1930*

The trees can be identified on the extreme right and extreme left of the scene. Between them stands a mutilated female figure, of which part of the bust, both arms and the head are missing. On her right stands a male figure of which only the legs remain. In the top corner, toward the left, the bust of another figure is visible, which the dimensions show to be male. On the head is a red attribute, widening out at the top, clearly an emblem of divinity or authority. This last figure is without arms (a *xoanon?*).

PLATE III

THE DECEASED HUNTING A HIPPOPOTAMUS

A fragment on linen cloth.   Height 6 in., width about 3 ¹/₂ in.
From the excavations of Giulio Farina in the necropolis of Gebelein, 1930

The figure of the hunter which is shown undamaged and in right profile, painted red, with black head and face, represents the deceased engaged in what has always been the most popular of Egyptian sports: hippopotamus hunting. The animal is recognizable from its big squat muzzle and short legs. The man, wearing a white loin-cloth knotted round his waist, is grasping a spear with which he is stabbing the back of the hippopotamus. A long curved appendage hangs down from his face, to which it is apparently connected: black and thick, with a red blob at the end, it cannot be identified with any degree of certainty.

PLATE IV

THE DECEASED FISHING

A fragment on linen cloth. Height about 7 7/8 in., width about 7 in.
From the excavations of Giulio Farina in the necropolis of Gebelein, 1930

The deceased is shown standing, with a red body and black head and face, and wearing a white loin-cloth knotted around his waist. He is stretching down his left arm, engaged in laying a peculiar kind of net (outlined in red and filled in with black) in the water, which is denoted by the conventional wavy lines. There must have been originally a long curved appendage hanging down from the man's face, in black, of the kind mentioned in the description of Plate III, and of which only the red blob at the end has remained clearly visible.

PLATE V

TWO LARGE SHIPS, WITH CABINS

*Fragments on linen cloth, with a broken outline. Height about 2 ft. 6 ³/₈ in., width about 4 ft. 5 in.
From the excavations of Giulio Farina in the necropolis of Gebelein, 1930*

Remnants of linen cloth, with a broken outline, have preserved this painting of two ships of different sizes, depicted in black, shown moving together, the crews of helmsmen and oarsmen seen in right profile.

The long oars, the helm, the cabin which is visible on the deck, and the oarsmen, are all painted red.

Starting from the first ship, which by the rules of Egyptian perspective is at the top, only the helmsman and a figure seated at the right centre of the ship are to be seen. In the second, in addition to the helmsman, four oarsmen are visible in the surviving left-hand portion. The identification of another male figure in the centre of the ship is uncertain. The badly damaged right-hand portion must have likewise contained an indeterminate number of oarsmen, as the presence of their oars on a surviving remnant testifies.

PLATE VI

DECORATED POTTERY BOWL

(PREDYNASTIC PERIOD KNOWN AS NAGADAH
ABOUT THE FIRST HALF OF THE 4th MILLENNIUM B.C.)

Height 2 $\frac{1}{2}$ in.; large diameter 5 $\frac{5}{16}$ in.; small diameter 4 $\frac{1}{2}$ in.
Purchased in Egypt. Catalogue supplement no. 1825

In heavy baked clay, covered both inside and out in red, the bowl rests on three of the four round legs which originally supported it. The rather thick off-white decoration coats only the inner, concave surface, and consists of a zigzag line just inside the rim, bordered by an unbroken circle within which are traced five hippopotami circling round one behind the other, from right to left, their squat shapes sketched rapidly yet expressively, filled in with vertical lines and two horizontal cross-lines; below, between the hippopotami, are five palm branches, the lower ends of which join in the centre to form a rough ellipse at the bottom of the bowl.

PLATE VII

TWIN POTTERY VASE

(PREDYNASTIC PERIOD, OF THE NAGADAH PHASE)

Light-weight baked clay vase. The round brim of one side is broken. Height 7 $^1/_8$ in.;
diameter of undamaged brim 2 in.; maximum diameter of each vase about 4 in.
Purchased in Egypt by Ernesto Schiaparelli. Catalogue supplement no. 1823

These two short-necked vases are the same shape; their sloping shoulders are linked by a hollow connection, so that they are inter-communicating; they are round and flat-bottomed. The outer surface is reddish-brown with rich reflections, on which geometrical designs have been traced in thick off-white paint, as well as a single scene encircling both vases which represents the attack of a crocodile on six goat-like animals and their defence by their owner armed with a bow and aided by four figures armed with spears.

The short necks of both vases are ornamented by the same motif of short vertical parallel lines. The sloping shoulders of the vases are decorated with a series of triangles, which on one vase point upward and on the other downward. Below, around the wide bowl of one of the vases (shown on the left in the plate) are five goats in profile, moving toward the right, tied together by a rope round their necks, the end of which is held in the hand of their owner, a man walking in front of them armed, as it appears, with a bow and arrow. A sixth goat is lying on the ground resting, and watching the others walk past. The large crocodile, seen not in profile but as though from above, is traced around the surface of the junction of the vases, and is turning round toward the right with its mouth open, in a direction which suggests not so much that it intends to attack the goats as that it wishes to take by surprise the four men who are standing in a line, looking off toward the right. The legs of these men are invisible. All the men are distinguished by an attribute on their heads (a feather?) and appear to be furnished with long curved appendages attached to their faces, visible in profile at the height of the nose, reminding us of other similar appendages noted on the male figures in Plates III, IV and V. Spears are resting on their shoulders, but not in readiness for attack.

The rest of the surface of the vase, down to the bottom, is covered with decorative motifs of interlocking triangles, pointing downward, and by patterns made up of short vertical, horizontal, oblique and herringbone lines, suggesting a string net designed for the carriage of the vase, or the basketwork of a cane or rush cradle.

Clues for the dating of the vase lie in the shape of the vase itself, a remarkable example of what W. M. Flinders Petrie has defined as " fancy forms; " in the thick white paint of the decoration; in the predominance of geometric decorative motifs; in the blocking in of the geometric figures and animals with a criss-cross of vertical and horizontal lines; in the imitation of a string net or rush basket for carrying and protecting the vase: all these elements make it possible to attribute or rather to assign the Turin twin vase to the earliest phase of the Egyptian predynastic period, known as Nagadah.

OLD KINGDOM

PLATE VIII

ROYAL STELA OF THE OLD KINGDOM
(END OF DYNASTY II)

Fragment of limestone stela, its whole remaining surface damaged. Height of remnant about 2 ft. 9 ¹/₂ in., width about 1 ft. 5 ³/₄ in.
From the excavations of Ernesto Schiaparelli in the area of the temple of the goddess Hathor in Gebelein, 1910. Catalogue supplement no. 12341

The left-hand portion of this stela was salvaged by Schiaparelli and brought to Turin. It is covered with sculpture in bas-relief, the work of a master, unfortunately now very badly damaged. Built into a wall of the temple of the goddess Hathor, it was necessary to cut it away from the upper portion which completed it, possibly because this was still more seriously impaired.

The slight obliquity of the left-hand border line, which gradually closes in as it slopes upward, shows that the stela had an arched top, reaching a height which contained the full figure of the king described below, for in the present state the entire bust, the head and the red or white royal head-dress, the infallible emblem of the high authority invested in the figure, are lacking.

The surface of this fragment of a stela is divided into two sections by the horizontal pictograph of the sky, ornamented with five-pointed stars. In the upper section remnants of a male figure are visible in right profile, whom his dimensions and accoutrements reveal as royal. All that has remained of this figure are the right arm from the elbow down, the right leg with a damaged foot which must have rested horizontally on the ground, and part of the left thigh. The sovereign is wearing a broad circular bracelet on his right wrist; in his hand he grasps four arrows, represented one beside the other. Naked, he wears around his waist a belt into which must be slipped the pear-shaped handle of the mace which protrudes from behind his left flank. From the same belt hangs down the long tail which reaches the ground close to his right leg.

Behind the figure of the king stand three figures of court officials, the two sculptured above being in reduced size; the first of these, in a better state, is in the same posture and attitude as the " sandal bearer " on the back of the famous palette for cosmetics in the Cairo Museum, which bears the name of Narmer. The third figure, sculptured below, is larger: that he is a young man of considerable importance is indicated by his special head-dress of which a long lappet hangs down on the right; by the garment of panther-skin girdling his hips, the tail of which he holds in his left hand; and by the instrument for writing on his right shoulder, the emblem of a scribe. In front of this figure are two hieroglyphs which W. Stevenson Smith reads as the uncommon proper name of Mut-nofre, but which can be read and interpreted in other equally acceptable ways.

In the lower section the reconstruction and the purpose of the figures is again uncertain, owing to the fact that both the right-hand portion and the bottom of the stela are missing. The latter loss, if we assume that this section was originally the same height as the one above, is considerable.

In spite of the damage, in the bottom left-hand corner the outlines of the royal boat are visible, distinguishable by the large ornament on the prow. The hieroglyphic inscription in the top right-hand corner is related to this: *šmśi (.u)-ḥru*; the same hieroglyphs and boat recur several times in the compartments on the front of the so-called " Palermo Stone, " recalling the passage every second year of the royal boat along the Nile through the whole of the land of Egypt.

At the top of the section, close to the border, is the name of a city, *Unu*, better known by the Greek denomination of Hermopolis in the Delta (or in Upper Egypt as Hermopolis Megale, capital of the 15th nome or southern district), followed by the hieroglyph of asps rearing up in a basket (*nb.t*). The inscription formed by the name of the city and the asps in a basket fails to lend itself to any clear interpretation: originally they must have been related to a hieroglyph, now badly damaged, which preceded the others, and of which only the fragment of a vertical line remains. Stevenson Smith suggests that the damaged hieroglyph might be read as *nṭr* = " god, " but this reading fails to stand up to careful scrutiny as being out of keeping with what follows and with the presence of the royal boat below, already qualified by its apposition.

The fragment of a stela reproduced in the plate records in the upper section either some event or some rite performed by the king; below we have a scene of royal activity, and the mention of a city which we know to have been in existence by the end of the Second Dynasty, about forty-eight hundred years ago: these records are of secondary importance in their incompleteness, or rather in the loss of some of those details which would have been so valuable if such an ancient monument had come down to us complete. Even in its present damaged state this fragment of a stela is still of undeniable value in connection with the figure of a king and events of which future discoveries may enable us to fill in the details, interpreting them with greater certainty.

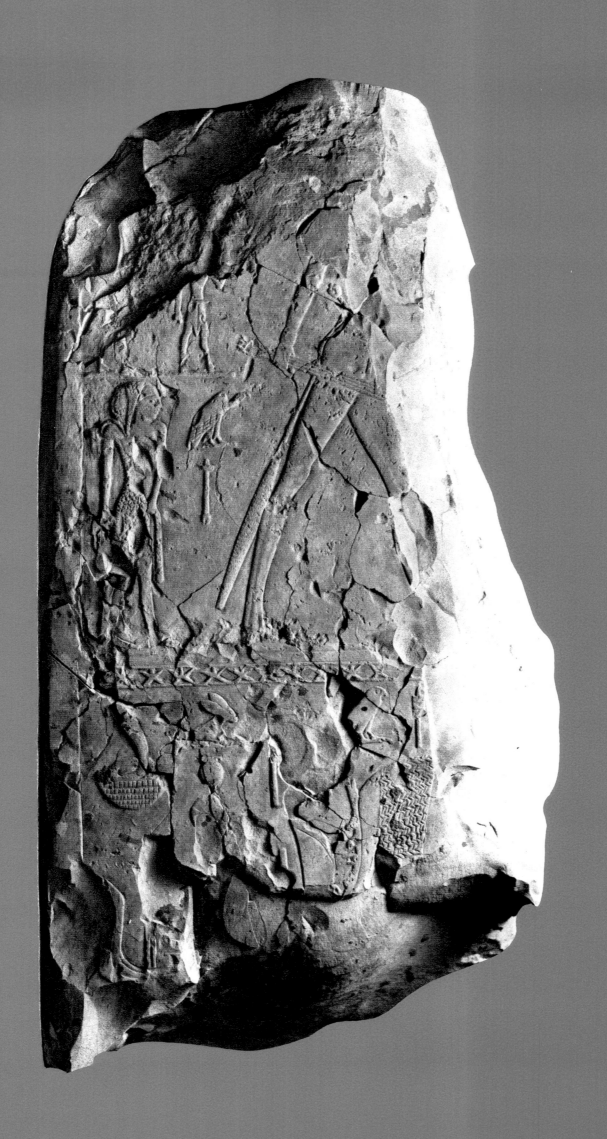

PLATE IX

THE ROYAL PRINCESS REDI-D

(OLD KINGDOM, DYNASTY III, about 2700-2620 B.C.)

Diorite statue.   Total height 2 ft. 8 ⁵/₈ in.; height of face from chin to hair-line 4 ⁷/₁₆ in.
Drovetti collection.   Catalogue no. 3065

The princess is seated on a chair reproducing the wooden seat of the period (in Egyptian, *ḥndu*), with four square-cut legs with curved wooden supports and a low back-rest.

The braids of her hair fall heavily onto her breast. She is wearing a linen calf-length dress. Both wrists are ornamented with bracelets. Her left forearm is folded under her breasts, with the hand open. The right hand rests on her right knee.

Her name and titles indicating her high lineage are legible on the flat top of the base, at the sides of her bare feet.

The only possible reading of the princess's name is found and perpetuated here: Redi-d, the reading *Redi-f* being untenable on account of the marked dissimilarity between the Egyptian *d* (= ⌐J', a cobra, *naja haie*) and *f* (= ✗⌣, a horned viper, *cerastes cornutus*).

No excavation has yet brought to light the body of the princess, nor is it possible, at the present state of our knowledge, to identify the members of her family.

PLATE X

Detail of Plate IX

PLATE XI

CASKET FOR WOMAN'S TOILET REQUISITES
(OLD KINGDOM)

Wooden casket. Height 7 1/2 in., including the legs which are 3 1/2 in. high, interconnected by cross bars; length 1 ft. 3 in., width 9 in. From the excavations of Ernesto Schiaparelli in the necropolis of Gebelein, 1914. Catalogue supplement no. 15709

The vertical wooden sides are lined on the outside with ivory facings, decorated with deep vertical ridges. Along the top of the facings runs a border made up of alternating light blue and black enamelled rectangles. The outer surface of the wooden lid is charmingly decorated with a motif consisting of two sets of four stylized lotus flowers, in blue and black enamel, in two rows, interset with five, four, and five alternating vertical strips of blue and black checks. The lotus flowers stand out on a background of ivory facings, skilfully held together by the enamels.

PLATE XII

STONE COSMETIC JARS
(OLD KINGDOM)

The height of the six small jars, from left to right, is 3 ¹/₂ in.; 1 ¹/₂ in.; 3 ⁵/₁₆ in.; 3 ¹/₈ in.; 2 ³/₈ in.; 1 ³/₄ in.
The diameter of the bowl is 7 ⁵/₈ in. From the excavations of Ernesto Schiaparelli in the necropolis of
Gebelein, 1910, 1911 and 1914

This plate reproduces six small stone jars of various shapes, together with a small round bowl with a raised border, all of which were designed to contain unguents or cosmetic ingredients. The height of the jars varies from 3¹/₂ inches in the case of the largest, which is the first on the left, to 1¹/₂ inches in the case of the smallest, the off-white, black-veined cylindrical jar. Women's fingers played gently around these jars some four thousand five hundred years ago.

The carefully chosen coloured stone of which they are fashioned, with its delicate web of variegated veining, adds to the beauty intrinsic in their minuteness, skilled workmanship and perfection of finish.

PLATE XIII

STATUETTE OF NUDE FEMALE FIGURE
(DYNASTY VI; BEGINNING OF MIDDLE KINGDOM)

Wooden statuette; nose and lips damaged, part of the right cheek and temple missing. Both arms, originally connected to the shoulder by wooden pins, have been lost. The wooden base is missing. Height 5 ⁵/₈ in. From the excavations of Ernesto Schiaparelli in Assiut, 1908. Catalogue supplement no. 8945

The silken surface of the wood, with its delicate effects of light and shade, add to the beauty of the sculpture of this young, clear-cut, slender body, rich in delicate variations, whether viewed from front, side or back. The extremely short hair, indicated in low relief, fits round the head like a helmet. The head is considerably damaged by tiny holes which cannot date back to the original artist. On the lobe of the left ear is a perforation for an earring.

MIDDLE KINGDOM

PLATE XIV

STATUETTE OF MENTUHOTEP
(END OF FIRST INTERMEDIATE PERIOD)

Wooden statuette. Height 2 ft. 8 ¹/₂ in.; including original base 3 ft. 2 ³/₄ in.
From the excavations of Ernesto Schiaparelli in Assiut, 1908. Catalogue supplement no. 8788

This is one of the two wooden statuettes of Mentuhotep which Schiaparelli took to Turin. The deceased is sculptured in the usual upright posture with his left leg forward, and grasping a long staff, now lost, in his left hand. The wooden sceptre '*b*', held horizontally in the right hand, is also missing.

On the head of the figure is the wig of the period, short, helmet-like, the plaits arranged horizontally in parallel lines of different lengths, descending in decreasing mass from the top of the head to the neck. Around his hips the deceased is wearing a white linen kilt, the colour revealed by traces of pigment still remaining at the back. The figure is barefoot.

The face is in an excellent state of preservation but the eyes, which were inlaid, have been lost. On the right breast between shoulder-blade and armpit is visible a piece of wood inserted by the original sculptor, and fixed in place by two wooden dowels. The finger nails were painted white. On the original base the name of the figure is legible: the " esteemed by the great god, *Mn.u-ḥtp* "

PLATE XV

COW AND CALF

(DYNASTY XI)

Wall painting in tempera, from the tomb of Iti, a high official. Measurements: height 1 ft. 9 $^1/_4$ in., width 2 ft. 7 $^1/_2$ in. From the excavations of Ernesto Schiaparelli in the necropolis of Gebelein, 1911

A charming subject from country life, observed by an unknown painter and portrayed some four thousand years ago on the wall of a private tomb in the district known today as Gebelein: a cow stretches out her muzzle to lick the back of a new-born calf with a gentle tongue.

PLATE XVI

ASS WITH DRIVER
(DYNASTY XI)

Wall painting in tempera from the tomb of Iti, a high official.   Height 1 ft. 4 $^1/_8$ in., width 2 ft. 3 $^1/_2$ in.
From the excavations of Ernesto Schiaparelli in the necropolis of Gebelein, 1911

The subject represents an ass bearing panniers of rush basket-work, full of corn, followed by his driver, making their way to the store-houses owned by Iti, the high official. It is one episode from a larger wall painting, in its present state 4 ft. 3 $^1/_4$ in. high and 7 ft. $^3/_4$ in. wide, in which an unknown Egyptian painter has represented the labour of men and animals employed in garnering the corn of the annual harvest.

This pleasant scene is visible in the bottom left-hand corner of the larger composition. The ass walks steadily onward toward the right, with even gait under the weight of its laden panniers. The left pannier, normally invisible, is represented by the painter upside down over the ass's back.

The driver keeps pace with the animal, a good stick grasped in his right hand and resting across his shoulder. Judging from the bloody sores which the painter has meticulously portrayed on the ass's hindquarters, it would seem that the driver had made good use of this same stick, and with no light hand!

PLATE XVII

THREE YOUTHS
ENGAGED IN MILITARY OR GYMNASTIC EXERCISES
(DYNASTY XI)

Wall painting in tempera, from the tomb of Iti, a high official.   Height 1 ft. 8 $^1/_8$ in., width 3 ft. 4 $^1/_2$ in.
From the excavations of Ernesto Schiaparelli in the necropolis of Gebelein, 1911

The subject, at the present state of our knowledge, is unique among
the decorative motifs of tombs.   In the wall fragment in question three
naked youths have been represented in left profile by the ancient painter,
with their eyes fixed ahead, on hands and knees.   The first seems to be
keeping his feet in the air, and the second and third to have their feet off
the ground and to be resting their right feet across their left legs.

The strange position of the legs of the first youth is to be found again
in another wall painting in Iti's tomb, where a woman is shown bending
in the same way over a typical stone corn-grinder: a position which is
both fatiguing and untenable.   In sculptures with the same subject, of which
a number are to be found in museums, the legs of the woman grinding
corn are always represented as resting on the ground.   This gives rise to a
hypothesis: may not the painter be intending to show the three youths
slant-wise?

Owing to the loss of the upper portion of the painting we are deprived
of the setting which might have contributed a background or explanation
for the action of the youths.   It is not possible to identify the lower part
of a yellow pole (?) at the extreme left of the painting as the support of a
canopy, because such supports were usually represented with polychromatic decorations.   This does not mean that it may not be taken to represent
a tree-trunk.   If this interpretation is accepted, the three youths would
appear to be engaged in an outdoor gymnastic or military exercise.   This
interpretation fits in with an official post held by Iti, as leader of the troops,
who are portrayed armed on another surviving portion of the tomb wall.

PLATE XVIII

HEAD OF A STATUE OF THE NOMARCH IBU
(DYNASTY XII)

Limestone head, reconstructed from fragments. The hair, forehead and cheek of the left side of the head are all badly damaged, as is the right eye. The nose is broken. Total height 10 in.; height from chin to hair-line 6 ¹/₄ in.; width from ear to ear 6 ⁷/₈ in. From the excavations of Ernesto Schiaparelli in Qau el Kebir, 1905-1906

This head of a statue has been for the most part reconstructed from fragments painstakingly collected by Schiaparelli from the tomb of the nomarch Ibu, situated in what is now the Arab district of Qau el Kebir. Ibu lived in the 12th dynasty, possibly during the reign of Sesostris III.

Traces of the original colouring remain in the black hair, stylized in a series of parallel undulating grooves, and in two black pupils, while red pigment is still partially visible on the face. Under the chin is a hole into which the ritual beard was inserted and attached to the face by straps, possibly strips of leather, shown by the sculptor in slight relief.

The face, sculptured with great art, its full volumes modelled with substantial and solid firmness within the oval line which bounds it, seems to lack something of humanity on account of the fixed and absent gaze.

PLATE XIX

RUNNING GAZELLE

(DYNASTY XI)

Limestone relief. Height 3 $^1/_{16}$ in., width 3 $^3/_4$ in.
From the excavations of Ernesto Schiaparelli in the necropolis of Gebelein, 1910
Catalogue supplement no. 12196

One of the most graceful fragments of figurative bas-relief decorating the temple of the goddess Hathor, of the 11th dynasty, in Gebelein in southern Egypt.

Running toward the right, on slender legs, a gazelle (*gazella dorcas*) stands out on the fragment in low relief, traced with a firm line and beautifully modelled.

NEW KINGDOM

PLATE XX

AMENHOTEP I

(SECOND KING OF DYNASTY XVIII, 1550-1528 B.C.)

Seated limestone statuette, in a good state of preservation, with some chips along the base. Total height 2 ft. 1 ⁵/₈ in.; height from chin to the border of the " nemes " 3 ¹/₂ in.; width of face from ear to ear 3 ¹/₁₆ in. Drovetti collection. Catalogue no. 1372

The figure of the king is seated on a cubic throne with back-rest. He is wearing the traditional linen head-dress *nemes* (*nms*), decorated with broad yellow and green stripes: on the front a hole is visible where the metal uraeus, or sacred asp, was originally inserted. The figure wears a ritual beard, in black, attached to the face by strips of leather, painted on the cheeks in black. A careful scrutiny reveals the thin red lines around the tips of the ears and the eyelids, guide lines for the work of the sculptor. Bust and feet are naked, and the figure is wearing the traditional close-pleated linen *scento* (Egyptian *šndw.t>šndy.t*, in Coptic *scent⁻*). The surfaces at the front of the throne and the top and front of the plinth are covered with the praenomen and name of the king, in their full official form.

The rounded shaping of the face of Amenhotep I recalls the facial types common in the statuary of a certain period of the 19th dynasty, so that the hypothesis has been advanced that the statuette was sculptured under the 19th dynasty.

The statuette was carried in procession on certain anniversaries of the Egyptian calendar.

Plate XXI

QUEEN AHMES-NOFRETARI

(SISTER AND WIFE OF KING AHMOSE, 1575-1550 B.C.;
MOTHER OF KING AMENHOTEP I, 1550-1528 B.C., OF DYNASTY XVIII)

*Wooden statuette. Height 1 ft. 5 in., including the original base, which is 9 ¹/₂ in. long, 3 ¹/₂ in. wide, 1 ³/₄ in. high
From the excavations of Ernesto Schiaparelli at Der el-Medîna, 1905. Catalogue supplement no. 6128*

This wooden statuette, gracefully and elegantly sculptured, is the work of a refined artist of the 19th dynasty. Ahmes-Nofretari is wearing a linen tunic down to her feet, and is bare-foot. A rich necklace is displayed around her neck. The lotus flower which the queen must have been holding in her right hand, has been lost.

Ahmes-Nofretari and her son Amenhotep I, who were deified after their deaths, were widely worshipped during the 18th, 19th and 20th dynasties. Their cult continued down to the Late Dynastic Period, being kept up particularly by the " servants in the Place of Truth, " the Egyptian denomination for those whose daily task it was to carry on the work in the Theban necropolis, in what is now the Arab centre of Der el-Medîna.

The statuette reproduced in the plate, as we can gather from the inscription on the top of the base and round its sides, was dedicated to the queen by two of the above-mentioned " servants " during the 19th dynasty.

PLATE XXII

TUTHMOSIS I

(THIRD KING OF DYNASTY XVIII, 1528-1510 B.C.)

Black granite seated statue, in excellent state of preservation. Total height 5 ft. 6 ¹/₈ in.;
height of face from chin to border of " nemes " 6 ¹/₈ in.; width from ear to ear 7 ¹/₄ in.
Drovetti collection. Catalogue no. 1374

Tuthmosis I, born out of wedlock, acquired the right to succeed his father Amenhotep I to the throne by marrying Ahmes, his half-sister, who was legitimate. He is here portrayed seated on a throne, naked except for the linen *scentō* round his hips. In his right hand he holds a folded cloth; his open left hand lies flat along the top of his left thigh. His bare feet rest on nine bows engraved on the flat top of the base, typifying Egyptian supremacy over nine neighbouring peoples, a symbolic representation dating back into the long-distant years of the Old Kingdom.

Much of the text engraved on the right side of the throne was erased at an early date. From the surviving inscription on the other side we learn that the statue was commissioned by his son, likewise illegitimate, Tuthmosis II, who took to wife the famous queen Hatshepsut.

On the top of the base, near the right foot, is the beginning of an inscription by J. Rifaud:

D^{rt} par J

which is to be found complete near the top of the right side of the throne:

D^{rt} par J^a Rifaud
sculpteur · a · thèbes
1818

PLATE XXIII

HEAD FROM STATUE OF THE GOD OSIRIS
(DYNASTY XVIII)

*Sandstone head. Height without two royal crowns 1 ft. 5 ³/₄ in.; from chin to border of white crown 1 ft. 3 ³/₈ in.;
width from ear to ear 1 ft. 4 ¹/₈ in. Drovetti collection. Catalogue no. 1387*

In the early years of the last century a huge and disproportionate crown, made up of the roughly assembled fragments of two unrelated Egyptian royal crowns, one white and one red, was placed on this head in Turin which is all that remains of a colossal statue of a deity. This head still possesses the damaged but precious remainder of its original and single crown, also white, and sculptured around the temples and brows to a height of 2 in. The photograph reproduces the head without the addition of the two artificial crowns. The remainder of the original crown is clearly visible but has never been pointed out until now.

The face, on which the original red colouring, characteristic of male figures, is still preserved, was at one time ornamented by a ritual beard.

This head, the work of a genuine artist of the middle of the 18th dynasty, passes on to posterity a number of innovations in respect of the contemporary sculpture and portrait tradition: the slight modulations of the facial planes, the gentle curves which give softness to the cheeks, the slight hollow forming a faint triangle between the eyes at the point where the nose joins the forehead. The lips too are more naturally and sensitively modelled. Their half-moon shape is not to be interpreted as a half-suppressed smile, a suggestion no longer held even in respect of ancient Greek statuary.

The absence of iconographical data makes it impossible to identify the head with any degree of certainty with any member of the 18th dynasty. More probably the head is all that has been found of the colossal statue of a deity, an Osiris, and the characteristic symbol of a white crown lends credence to this view.

The back view of the head is carefully flattened, which suggests that the statue, in its pristine form, was designed to stand against a flat surface such as the wall of one of the famous temples of the period.

PLATE XXIV

TUTHMOSIS III

(SIXTH KING OF DYNASTY XVIII, 1490-1436 B.C.)

Black granite seated statue. Height 6 ft. 3 ¹/₂ in. Drovetti collection. Catalogue no. 1376

Immortalized by the artist who re-created the king in superb beauty, he sits on his throne in a solemn and imperial pose. On his head he wears the linen *nemes* ornamented by a uraeus. Naked from the waist up, he is wearing a *scento* round his hips. Both hands rest flat, palms downward, on his thighs. His bare feet rest on nine bows, engraved on the top of the base (the symbolism is explained in the description of Plate XXII).

A born leader, Tuthmosis III successfully planned and fought a number of campaigns in Asia, recorded in the Tacitus-like lines of his " Annals " which list the cities conquered, the vast spoils carried home, the heavy tributes exacted from Assyria, Babylonia, Mitanni and the island of Cyprus. . . . In imitation of an earlier Tuthmosis he erected a stela on the banks of the conquered Euphrates. The tallest of the obelisks in Rome today, standing in the square of St. John's Lateran, is a testimonial to his name.

On the front of the base is the following inscription by J. Rifaud:

DÈCOUVEt PAR

J.�q RifAud

SculptEUR AU CERVICE DE

[C corrected later to S]

Mᴿ DROVEtti A thEbES. 1818

PLATE XXV

Detail of Plate XXIV

PLATE XXVI

AMENHOTEP II

(SEVENTH KING OF DYNASTY XVIII, 1436-1413 B.C.)

Red granite statue, broken at the waist, with beard, right forearm and both ankles damaged.
The front of the vertical surface at the left of the base is likewise damaged. Total height 4 ft. 11 $^7/_8$ in.;
height of the face from chin to border of the " nemes " 6 $^3/_4$ in.; width from ear to ear 7 $^1/_8$ in.
Drovetti collection. Catalogue no. 1375

The Egyptian sculptor has represented the king kneeling, resting back on his heels, offering to a deity two spherical libation vases full of wine. He is wearing a linen head-dress or *nemes*, with uraeus. A ritual beard is attached to his chin, fastened by strips of leather sculptured in low relief on the cheeks. Around the hips is a linen garment or *scento*. The feet are bare.

The sculptor, even while repeating a traditional type of statue of which the oldest example dates back to the Old Kingdom, has shown great art and skill in dominating the difficult material in which he is working and has shaped the red granite into a vigorous youthful figure with an exquisite play of light and shade. The face of the king, fixed in religious concentration on the priestly act he is performing, is both graceful and grave.

Amenhotep II, besides the cares of government and successful military exploits, was fond of sport. His passion for archery, sailing and riding are recorded on a stela which can still be seen between the paws of the Sphinx of Giza.

PLATE XXVII

Detail of Plate XXVI

SPHINX

(DYNASTY XVIII)

A sandstone statue. Length 9 ft. 10 in., height 4 ft. 9 ⁷/₈ in., width 2 ft. 10 ⁵/₈ in.
The face from the chin to the border of the " nemes " is 10 ¹/₄ in. high, 1 ft. 1 in. wide from ear to ear.
Drovetti collection. Catalogue no. 1408

The Egyptian Museum of Turin possesses two sandstone sphinxes, powerfully sculptured, showing the face of Amenhotep III (1405-1367 B.C.) (Plate XXIX). The sphinx here reproduced is the one which is better preserved, and was found, as the inscription given below testifies, by Jacques Rifaud.

In the space on the front of the *nemes* there must originally have been a uraeus, which has since been lost. On the right flank the diminutive figure of a standing deity holding a sceptre, is visible, engraved in left profile.

Amenhotep III, who declared that he was the mortal son of Amon, the god of the dynasty, as shown by the theogonic text which was prepared for the dual purpose of commemoration and propaganda, had an easy reign. He had no cause to intervene by force in the Asiatic territories under Egyptian rule. His days were spent in the tranquil atmosphere of a true " Magnifico " of the 11th century B.C., devoted to the erection of harmonious monuments, to the hunting of aurochs and lions, to contracting marriages with Asiatic princesses and to enriching the royal harem with beautiful women, also from Asia.

On the shoulder of the sphinx's front leg is the engraving by J. Rifaud:

Dᵗ par Jᵃ Rifaud
sculptEUR
1818
Thèbes
AU SERVICE D. M
Drovetti

PLATE XXX

AMON-RA, GOD OF THEBES, AND KING TUT-ANKH-AMON
(DYNASTY XVIII)

Limestone group. Total height 6 ft. 11 in., width 3 ft. ⁵/₈ in.;
height of the face of the king from chin to border of the " nemes " 4 ⁵/₈ in.; width from ear to ear 5 ¹/₂ in.
Drovetti collection. Catalogue no. 768

On the left of the group is the seated figure of Amon-Ra, recognizable by his flat head-dress with two tall stylized feathers. In his left hand he grasps the *'nḥ* amulet. On his left stands the figure of Tut-ankh-amon (1347-1339 B.C.), less than life-size, his right arm embracing the shoulder of the god. The king, bare-footed like the god Amon-Ra, is wearing the linen head-dress or *nemes* with a uraeus, and a tightly pleated linen garment, one fold of which hangs down in front in the form of a triangle.

The face of the king deserves recognition as an excellent example of 18th dynasty portraiture which, although marked by a characteristic tendency to idealize the subject, could yet reveal minute observation of the more important iconographic details. All the characteristic features of Tut-ankh-amon are to be found in the face of the statue in question: his long, triangular-shaped face, his curved upper lip turning down at the corners, his thick protruding lower lip; the cut of his mouth, not in a straight line but slightly irregular. The same features are to be found in the other effigies of the king, in the best statues, in the portrait head of the gold mask and in his gold sarcophagus at the Cairo museum. It follows that the name of Horemheb, the last ruler of the 18th dynasty, which is inscribed on both sides of the front of the throne on which Amon-Ra is seated, and to be seen again in the two lines of inscription above the king, unquestionably reveals a later utilization on the part of Horemheb of this group of statuary. It was begun under Tut-ankh-amon but not completed, possibly because of the brevity of his reign.

The present group is of historical importance if it was sculptured, as appears probable, after the restoration of the cult of the dynastic and national god Amon-Ra, a restoration effected by Tut-ankh-amon after the interim during which Amenhotep IV (Akhenaten) had impelled his subjects to worship Aten as god of the dynasty.

On the right-hand side of the throne, at the top, is an unfinished inscription by J. Rifaud:

N. I

Dᵗ PAR Jᵃ Rifaud

sculptEUR

1818

Thèbes

AU SERVIÇE D. M.

D

PLATE XXXI

Detail of Plate XXX

PLATE XXXII

HOREMHEB AND MUTNODME

(DYNASTY XVIII)

Portion of group of statuary in black granite. The right breast and left forearm of the queen are damaged.
Total height 4 ft. 2 ³/₄ in., width 2 ft. 11 in.; height of the damaged face of the queen,
from chin to wig 5 ¹/₈ in.; width of face from ear to ear 6 ¹/₈ in.
Drovetti collection. Catalogue no. 1379

On the left of this group of statuary, seated on a high-backed throne, is the headless figure of Horemheb, the last king of the 18th dynasty (1335-1308 B.C.). He must have been wearing the *nemes* or linen head-dress, of which the two lappets are still visible falling over his shoulders onto his breast. In his right hand the king is holding the *ḥq*ʾ sceptre, his left hand, resting on his left thigh, holds the ʿnḫ amulet. By his side sits the queen Mutnodme embracing her husband, her right arm placed around his waist, while her left hand rests flat along the top of her left leg.

The queen is wearing a necklace and earrings. Her head is covered by the wig worn at the time, on which rests the so-called *modius*, on the front of which the remnants of two uraei can still be seen. Both king and queen are barefoot.

On the king's side of the throne two Nubian and two Asiatic prisoners, their arms tied behind their backs, have been lightly engraved. The other side of the throne has been divided horizontally into two partitions: the upper shows a winged female sphinx lying, raising the forelimbs shaped like human arms to do homage to the name of the queen inscribed in the cartouche. In the lower partition are seven tall-stemmed and six shorter-stemmed lotus flowers.

On the rear of the throne is a long text, engraved horizontally in twenty-seven mutilated lines, referring to the coronation of Horemheb.

PLATE XXXIII

GOD PTAH OF MEMPHIS
(DYNASTY XVIII)

Black granite statue.   Total height 6 ft. 9 ¹/₈ in.
The face of the god from chin to border of head-dress is 7 ¹/₈ in. high ; width 7 ³/₈ in., measured from ear to ear.
Drovetti collection.   Catalogue no. 86

A fine example of statuary, larger than life-size, representing the god " beautiful of face " worshipped at Memphis, standing in his characteristic xoanon or mummiform posture.   He is wearing a smooth, close-fitting head-dress, low over his brows; a rich necklace encircles his neck.   In each hand he grasps an ʿnḥ amulet, and he holds along his body the ḏḏ column and wꜣs sceptre, signifying his life-power, duration and dominion.   He is wearing a ritual beard, attached to the chin by two strips of leather carved on the cheeks in low relief.

The statue was dedicated to Ptah by Amenhotep III, a king of the 18th dynasty (1405-1367 B.C.), whose name can be read on the pedestal in the line of writing engraved at the feet of the god.

On the left side of the base is the inscription cut by J. Rifaud, which is reproduced on the second page of the Preface.

PLATE XXXIV

STATUE OF A GODDESS

(DYNASTY XVIII)

A mutilated statue, broken off at the knees and with parts of both arms missing. Total height 4 ft. 11 $^7/_8$ in.
Height of face from chin to wig 5 $^1/_2$ in.; width from ear to ear 6 $^1/_4$ in.
Drovetti collection. Catalogue no. 694

The goddess, recognizable as such by the solar disk between two cow's horns on her head, and the uraeus on her brows, is represented standing upright, grasping the *w3s* sceptre in her left hand, and holding the *'nḫ* amulet in her right hand, which rests along her right side. She is wearing a close-fitting linen tunic, held up by two straps over her shoulders. The sculptor has represented her with two ornamental rosettes on her breasts. A rich necklace encircles her neck, and on her wrists are bracelets.

Another similar statue, of a different period, which is housed in the Château Borély at Marseilles, is today identified with Isis. In respect of this Turin statue, which in the past was considered to be a Hathor or an Isis–Hathor, Jacques Vandier has recently suggested (in 1958) identifying her as the Theban goddess Mut: an identification which was first proposed, without any reasons being given, by Pier-Camillo Orcurti in his once-famous *Catalogo illustrato dei Monumenti Egizi del R. Museo di Torino* (Turin, 1852, vol. I, p. 43, no. 6).

PLATE XXXV

MAN AND WIFE OF THE NEW KINGDOM
(BEGINNING OF DYNASTY XVIII FROM 1575 B.C.)

A diorite group. Height 11 ¹³/₁₆ in. Purchased by Ernesto Schiaparelli in Egypt, from a dealer.
Catalogue supplement no. 1219

The man—a priest, as we learn from the two vertical lines of inscription on the back of the group—is holding the right hand of the woman in his left. Not much taller than his wife, he has a bald head and wears a short, knee-length kilt. His wife, much younger than her husband, is wearing an ankle-length close-fitting linen tunic. Her heavy hair, not separated into braids, is worn in the fashion of the beginning of the 18th dynasty, and frames her face symmetrically, falling loosely over her shoulders. The bare hands and feet of both husband and wife are undeniably coarse in shape. The left arm of the woman, hanging down her side, is considerably longer than the right.

The group, which is in an excellent state of preservation, was commissioned by the son of the deceased, likewise a priest. With its charming suggestion of intimacy, it is a good example of the art of the early 18th dynasty, although there still remain traces characteristic of the Middle Kingdom.

PLATE XXXVI

STATUE OF ONEN
(DYNASTY XVIII)

A syenite statue, height 4 ft. 9 ¹/₂ in.   Drovetti collection.   Catalogue no. 1377

The brother of Queen Tiy, wife of King Amenhotep III (18th dynasty, 1405-1367 B.C.), Onen, filled high offices both at Court and in the ecclesiastical hierarchy, as we learn from the two columns of inscription on the plinth behind the statue.

The figure stands upright, his arms hanging down by his sides, and is wearing a long calf-length garment; above he wears the skin of an animal, ornamented with stylized stars, as befits his high degree in the priesthood. From his right side hang three metal chains, and a peculiarly shaped container which has been identified as a container or bag for instruments used by the astronomers of the period. Just below the belt, among the chains, is a royal cartouche bearing the name of Amenhotep III, spelt backwards.

PLATE XXXVII

UNIDENTIFIED HEAD
(DYNASTY XVIII-XIX)

A grey quartzite head with damaged nose, right eyebrow and ears.
Total height 9 ¹/₁₆ in.; height of face from chin to forehead 6 ¹/₄ in.; width from ear to ear 6 ³/₄ in.
Catalogue no. 3141

This head was part of a statue sculptured in the New Kingdom, of a person who is now nameless. The features are those of a man no longer young, with a beardless face, a shaven head without wig, a wide forehead and dolichocephalic skull (see Plate XXXVIII). In profile the curve of the cranium is continued or rather echoed in the curve of the eyebrows and eyelids, which the sculptor seems to have deliberately magnified. The straight-cut lips stand out from the soft, full cheeks. This head is the work of a gifted artist who used such extreme simplicity of means to model a face with elegance and clarity.

Plate XXXVIII

Profile of the unidentified head in Plate XXXVII

PLATE XXXIX

STATUETTE OF TA-NEFERT
(DYNASTY XVIII)

Limestone statuette. Height 8 ¹/₁₆ in. Drovetti collection. Catalogue no. 3094

Seated statuette of a deceased lady named Ta-nefert (*t3 nfr.t*), on a square, backless seat. She is wearing the white linen tunic of the period, down to her bare feet. A rich necklace encircles her neck, and she is wearing bracelets on her wrists. Her face is overshadowed by the abundant black plaits of her wig, which cover her shoulders and fall heavily down to her breasts. The blackness of her hair emphasizes by contrast the luminous whiteness of the tranquil face of this young woman. Her hands rest palm downward along her legs in a somewhat cold, conventional pose.

PLATE XL

THE GIRL NEFRTMAU
(DYNASTY XVIII)

Wooden statuette. Height 8 $^1/_{16}$ in. Drovetti collection. Catalogue no. 3107

A slim figure, Nefrtmau stands before us with the candid air of a girl on the threshold of adolescence, her slight arms hanging down by her sides, in the stereotyped pose of funerary statuettes.

Her hair is arranged as she chose to wear it during her life-time. Round her waist is a golden loin-cloth and she is wearing a gold necklace round her neck.

The wooden base of the statuette is original. From the inscription on this base we learn that the statuette was dedicated to Nefrtmau by her mother Neb.t-hotop.

FOREWORD TO PLATES XLI–XLIX

In February 1906 Ernesto Schiaparelli cleared away the piles of débris and penetrated into the blocked entrance of a tomb hewn out of the rock in the mountainous district of the Theban necropolis, known by the Arab name of Der el-Medîna.

This tomb, which had remained inviolate and undisturbed for thousands of years, housed the remains of Khai in his two wooden sarcophagi, of which one was covered with gold and both were enclosed in a huge bitumen-covered box. The tomb also contained the remains of his wife, Mry.t, in a single gold-covered wooden coffin, perhaps prepared originally for the husband who outlived her, likewise enclosed in a bitumen-covered box. Funerary equipment, including a papyrus copy of the so-called " Book of the Dead" (see Plate XLIX), furniture, cloth and linen clothing, toilette articles and everyday objects, household utensils and food supplies, etc., make up the spoils of this remarkable and precious find.

Khai (see Plates XLI, XLII, XLIII) lived in the reigns of Amenhotep II (1436-1413 B.C.), of Tuthmosis IV (1413-1405 B.C.) and of Amenhotep III (1405-1367 B.C.), who were respectively the seventh, eighth and ninth kings of the 18th dynasty. He occupied the posts of officer of State and director of works in the necropolis of Der el-Medîna.

Some of the children of Khai and Mry.t are visible in the scenes of family life which decorate the outer walls of wooden chests in which cloth and clothing were stored (see Plate XLIV).

There is no evidence that the ancestors of Khai were among the leading families of the period. The silence of the relevant documents known to us is significant in this respect. In some chapters of the copy of the " Book of the Dead" discovered in the tomb, we read the name of the father with no mention of the offices he held or of the services he had rendered. Also the silence of the documents in connection with Mry.t leads us to advance the hypothesis that she probably belonged to one of the many middle-class families of the period.

PLATE XLI

STATUETTE OF KHAI

Wooden statuette standing on original base, with no inscription.
Height 1 ft. 4 7/8 in. From the excavations of Ernesto Schiaparelli at Der el-Medina, 1906.
Catalogue supplement no. 8335

The statuette, in very hard wood which has taken on a deep brown colour over the years, represents Khai standing, his left foot forward, his arms stretched along his sides, wearing the linen garment of the time, from the waist down to below the knees. The vertical line of writing down the front of the garment expresses the hope that all the offerings placed on the table of offerings of Amon, king of the gods, should be for the *Ka* (1) of the director of works in the necropolis of Thebes, the justified Khai.

On his head the figure is wearing a wig of tight parallel plaits, which spreads out gently overshadowing his shoulders.

The undamaged statuette is the work of a highly sensitive artist, who has represented Khai in his prime with a rich variety of modulating tones and shades. The lightness of touch seems to add lustre to the wooden surface, polished by the artist with loving care.

In conformity with the burial customs of the time, the statuette was found placed on the high-backed wooden chair, painted in black and in an excellent state of preservation, which formed part of the funerary ornaments of the tomb of Khai and his wife.

(1) The *Ka* (*K*) was considered as the *dynamis* or vital power of the individual to whom it was attached both in life and in death. It was strictly associated with the funerary statue of the deceased and with the *post mortem* provisions for nourishment by the funerary priests or relatives of the deceased, or by offerings on the altar of a god.

PLATE XLII

Side view of the statuette in Plate XLI

PLATE XLIII

Back view of the statuette in Plate XLI

PLATE XLIV

FUNERARY CHEST FOR CLOTHING

A wooden chest, with four square-cut feet. Height 1 ft. 2 ⁹/₁₆ in., width 1 ft. 1 in., length 1 ft. 6 ⁷/₈ in.
From the excavations of Ernesto Schiaparelli at Der el-Medina, 1906

The plate reproduces a scene painted on the principal side of one of the wooden chests in the funerary furniture of Khai and his wife Merit. Used for storing linen, it is rectangular in form with a sloping roof-shaped lid, the remaining sides decorated with geometric patterns, rosettes and imitations of wooden veining, admirable in their bright colouring.

The subject of the scene reproduced, which is related to the funerary cult, was painted hurriedly on purpose for the occasion, which accounts for the omissions indicated below.

On the right sit both Khai and his wife, on a four-legged high-backed chair with a wide seat, painted in black. Under the wife's side of the chair stand two articles for her toilet. On the left of the scene, separated from husband and wife by a one-legged table covered with food, stand two of their children, a girl and a youth. Their names should have been written in the two spaces prepared for vertical writing which have been left blank above the two figures. In their right hands they hold respectively a small aspergillum vase and a lotus flower. Two of the seven lines of vertical text written in black over the heads of the seated deceased give the name of Merit, two that of Khai, while three repeat the standard text of the funerary formula for offerings in the name of the god Osiris. The same formula recurs also in the horizontal text, which is beautifully written along the upper border of the front top of the lid, in the names of the deities Amon-Ra and Hathor.

The hurried tracing of the inscriptions in the aforementioned seven vertical lines is worthy of note, and the disorderly way in which some of the characters are turned first to the right, then to the left. The figures are also roughly drawn, all of the same height. Their faces show no attempt at individualization or portraiture. The scene as a whole is depicted along the traditional lines laid down for these scenes, such as have been endlessly repeated.

The cord, of which the ends still remain tied to the two wooden knobs on the top right-hand end of the lid and on the vertical side of the chest below, was cut by the discoverer in order to learn the contents of the chest.

PLATE XLV

A VASE FROM THE TOMB OF KHAI

Heavy clay vase. Height 1 ft. 3 in.
From the excavations of Ernesto Schiaparelli at Der el-Medina, 1906

The long cylindrical neck is half the total height of the vase and is joined to a globular body terminating in a flat annular base. To the shoulders of the vase, hurriedly ornamented with a pattern raying out in dark brown, light brown and green on a white ground, are attached two thick handles decorated with boughs and green leaves, one on each side of the vase.

The decoration of the neck, brightly coloured and in an excellent state of preservation, has been painted on fine linen. It consists of two yellow *nfr* pictographs on either side of another in white, resting on a black *nb* pictograph meaning " Every good! "; over these is depicted in black the great *udjat* eye to ward off evil spirits, its brightness enhanced by the white of the eyeball (Plate XLVI).

This decorative motif, which is repeated on the other side of the neck, is enclosed both on the right and the left by two flourishing fronds of light green papyrus, possibly an allusion to and symbol of the Delta district from whence came the liquid contained in the vase (Plate XLVII).

The cover of the circular mouth is still intact today, fastened with straps of linen passed back and forth across the lid and around the neck.

Plate XLVI

Detail of Plate XLV

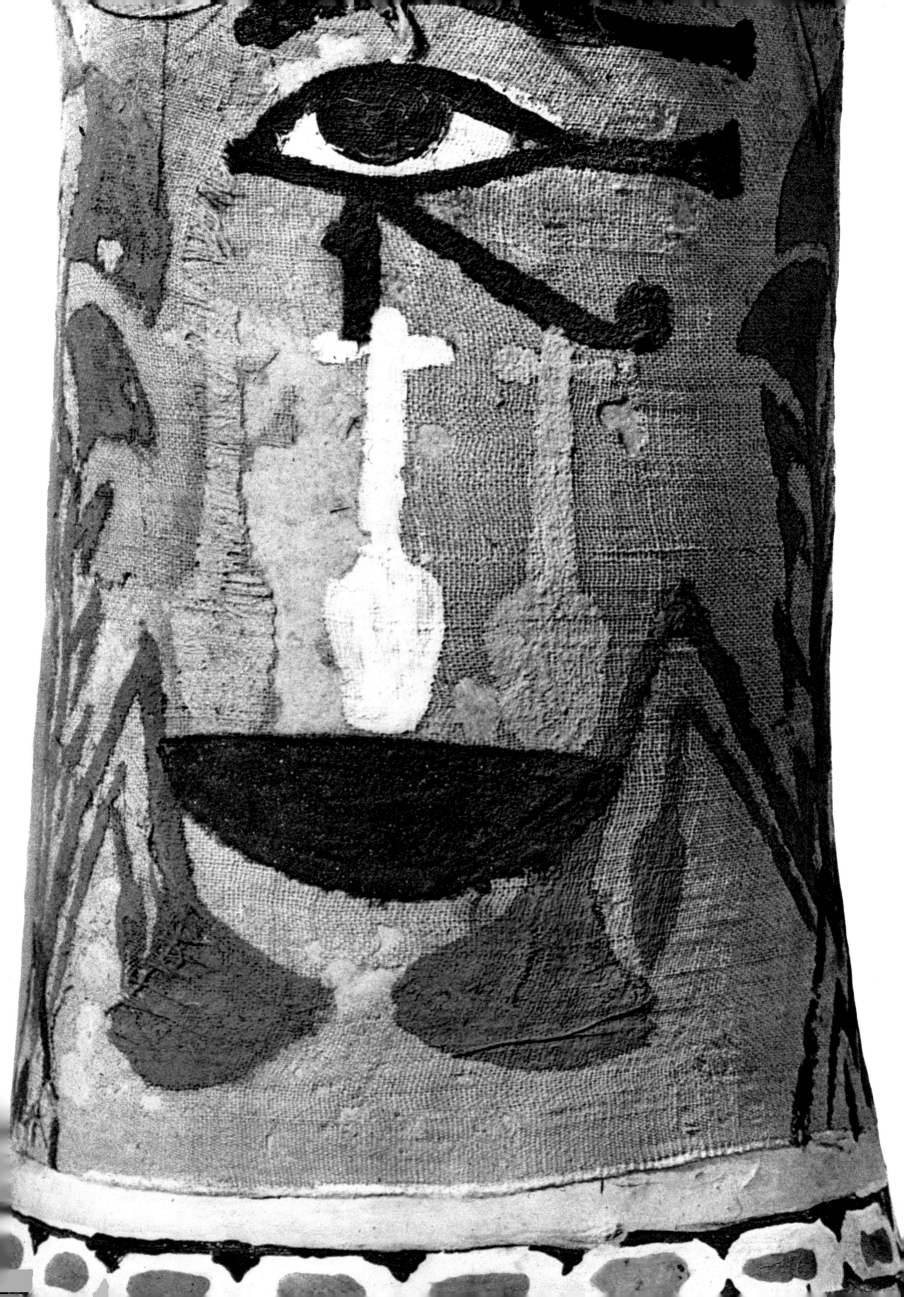

PLATE XLVII

Side view of vase in Plate XLV

PLATE XLVIII

A VASE FROM THE TOMB OF KHAI

Heavy clay vase. Height 1 ft. 4 $^1/_8$ in.
From the excavations of Ernesto Schiaparelli at Der el-Medîna, 1906

The cylindrical neck of this vase is taller than the one reproduced in
Plate XLV. It is covered with fine linen cloth and decorated with eight
horizontal zig-zag lines alternately green and black. Another zig-zag line,
black on a white ground, marks the base of the neck.

The mouth of the vase is still sealed by the same method described in
connection with the preceding vase. The white painted shoulders of the
vase are decorated with a petal design, painted roughly in alternate green
and black interspersed by light brown half-petals. This decoration is
bordered at the bottom by a circular line of green dots.

This vase likewise has two strong handles on opposite sides, decorated
with alternate black, white, and green stripes.

The base of the vase is flat and annular.

PLATE XLIX

KHAI AND HIS WIFE MERIT

On the left stand Khai and his wife, both in right profile, rendering homage to the god Osiris. The god sits on a low-backed throne, wearing on his head the ꜣtf crown and holding in his hands the wꜣs and ḥqꜣ sceptres, the latter with a volute top, and a flagellum. Over the god's throne is a canopy supported by lotus flower capitals, on the roof of which rear thirteen uraei with solar disks on their heads.

Between the deceased and the god stands a table bearing their offerings of food and flowers.

This scene, of which the colours are still fresh and bright three thousand five hundred years after it was painted, opens the papyrus of the so-called "Book of the Dead" in the name of Khai, measuring about 46 feet. It is one of the oldest to be found *in situ*. The text, in cursive hieroglyphics, was written by an able scribe of the period. It is ornamented by scenes in many colours, decorating the different "chapters."

A copy of this "Book" in the name of Merit, which also makes frequent mention of Khai, was donated to the Bibliothèque Nationale of Paris in 1862 by De Luynes, and is housed in the Cabinet des Médailles.

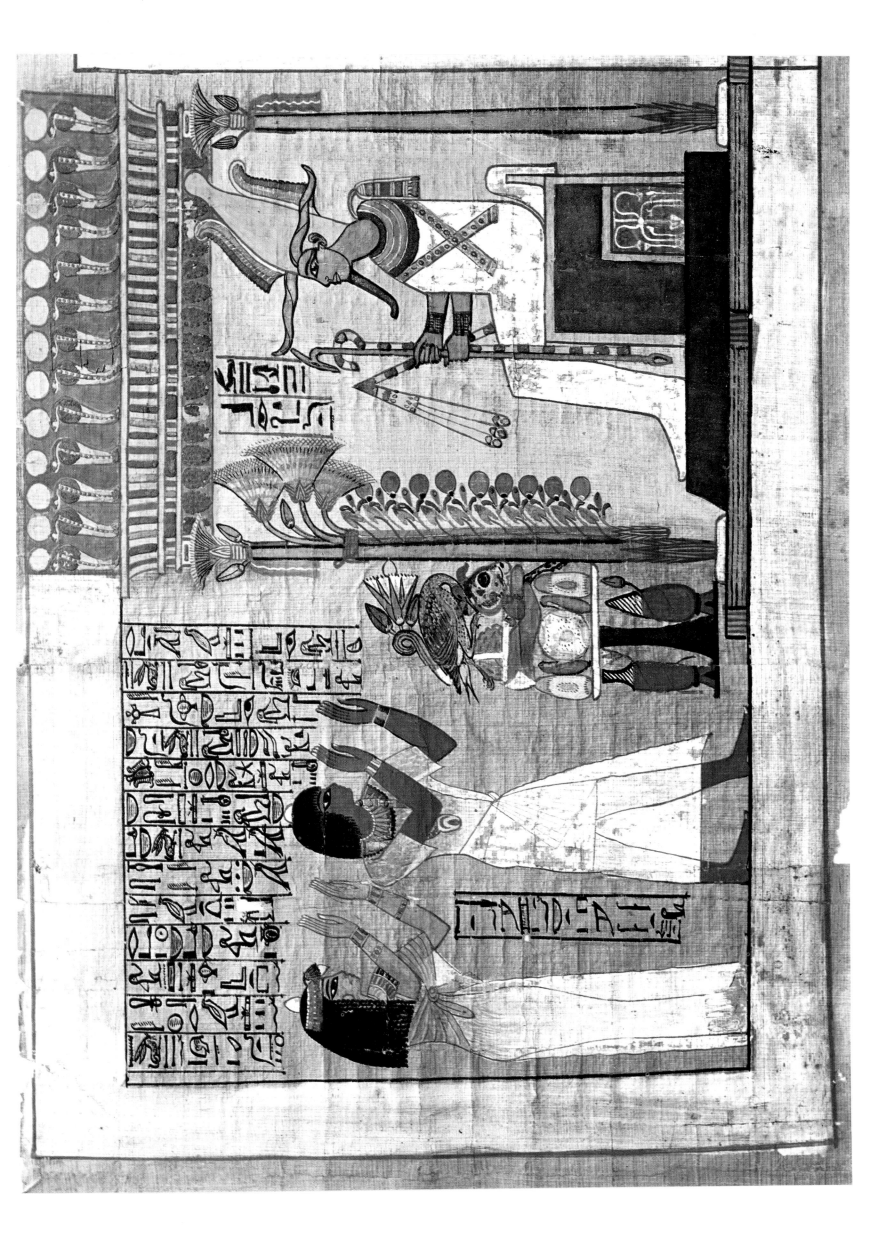

FOREWORD TO PLATES L–LII

In the zone of the modern Der el-Medîna (the necropolis of Thebes on the west bank of the Nile) Ernesto Schiaparelli discovered in 1905 the tomb of the painter May, consisting of three chambers of modest dimensions. The scenes in tempera on the walls of these chambers and the roof of one of them, carefully detached the following year by Fabrizio Lucarini, the Luccan restorer who deserves mention here, were remounted in Turin with all due caution and now line the small chamber opening off along the left wall just inside Exhibition Room III, where today they form one of the many attractions of the Museum.

Here some of the best-preserved details are reproduced. A stela in May's name, part of the Drovetti collection, was in the Museum's possession long before Schiaparelli discovered the tomb, and is described in the Museum catalogue, compiled by A. Fabretti, F. Rossi, and R. V. Lanzone, under entry no. 1579. Another smaller stela of May is known to be in existence, and is today in the possession of the W. J. Bankes collection at Kingston Lacy (near Wimborne, Dorset); on this the deceased is reproduced reciting a hymn in praise of Ra, the sun god.

The dating of May's tomb is thought to be about the end of the 18th dynasty.

PLATE L

A HUSBAND AND WIFE

Tempera wall painting. Maximum height of fragment 1 ft. 8 ⁷/₈ in., width 1 ft. 3 in.
From the excavations of Ernesto Schiaparelli at Der el-Medîna, 1905

The painting reproduced in the plate is displayed on the end wall of the small room mentioned in the foreword. It shows a woman, the " lady of the house " Mut-nofre, and her husband, whose name must have figured in the missing portion of painted wall above his head. They are seated on a wide high-backed wooden chair of the period, with four claw-footed legs, of which the Museum possesses a counterpart, mentioned in the description of Plate XLI.

The deceased, who are portrayed as having almost the same height, are wearing pomade cones on their black wigs. These cones were widely used by the living during the New Kingdom and were attributes also of the deceased, when these were reproduced as living and moving.

Mut-nofre is wearing a long, full tunic of white linen, leaving one breast bare. Sitting on her husband's right, her left arm is placed around his waist and her right hand is resting on his left arm.

These two figures are the parents of May. His wife and children are portrayed and their names inscribed on the stela mentioned in the foreword, which is in the possession of the Museum, under catalogue no. 1579.

PLATE LI

THE MOURNERS

Fragment of a tempera wall painting, with a broken outline. Height 1 ft. 2 $^9/_{16}$ in., width 11 $^1/_4$ in.
From the excavations of Ernesto Schiaparelli at Der el-Medîna, 1905.

This fragment shows the figures of seven women (the black hair of an eighth is visible on the extreme left), portrayed in left profile and dressed in white tunics. The painter has realistically grouped them in various animated attitudes of grief, participants in a funeral ceremony.

Care has been taken in representing the loose-falling hair, and the artist has carried his love of detail to the point of painting the finger-nails and the tears that fall one after another from their eyes.

PLATE LII

DECORATION OF TOMB CEILING IN TEMPERA

Painting in tempera. Measurements of detail reproduced in plate: length 1 ft. 11 ¹/₂ in., width 2 ft. 7 ¹/₂ in. From the excavations of Ernesto Schiaparelli at Der el-Medîna, 1905

The plate reproduces very clearly a detail of the ceiling decoration in May's tomb. Two different decorative motifs are used, separated by a yellow band on which a funerary text is inscribed in green, mentioning the god Aten " who rests in life in the horizon. " The right side of the ceiling is adorned with blue rosettes in which eight white lines ray out from a red centre, each rosette ringed round by a buff-coloured border, alternating with white interlacing whorls. On the opposite side of the ceiling the decoration consists of a series of parallel zig-zag stripes in the following order of colours: blue, green, red, green, blue; and two rows of yellow rhomboids, touching at the corners, each of which contains a red four-petalled flower.

This decoration was presumably intended as an imitation of the textiles with which ceilings were generally covered at the time.

PLATE LIII

STELA OF THE DECEASED MEKY MONT
(DYNASTY XVIII)

Limestone stela. Height 11 ¹/₄ in., width 7 ⁷/₈ in.
From the excavations of Ernesto Schiaparelli at Der el-Medîna, 1909. Catalogue supplement no. 9492

Below two large *udjat* eyes, one on either side of the *šn* ring, of which the meaning is not clear, sit the deceased Meky Mont on the left, raising a lotus flower to his face, and his wife Neb-m-uśh.t, on the wide wooden high-backed chair of the time, similar to the chair of the deceased in Plate L. On the right stands the brother of the deceased, sprinkling with holy water the food offered on a one-legged table.

The two lines of text below contain the usual funerary formula, inscribed from right to left: it invites the god Osiris " Lord of Abydos, great god, sovereign of eternity " to grant Meky Mont " oxen, fowls, every good pure offering by which the god lives. "

The two male figures, characterized by the red colouring of their skin, wear short linen kilts over which hangs a longer, more transparent garment, also of linen, through which the kilt is visible. The woman, painted in the traditional yellowish shade, is wearing a linen tunic with shoulder-straps.

The entire background of the scene is blue, according to the current fashion at the beginning of the 18th dynasty.

PLATE LIV

DANCER

(DYNASTY XVIII)

Limestone ostrakon with irregular outline. Maximum width 4 1/8 in., length 6 5/8 in.
Drovetti collection. Catalogue no. 7052

On the front of the roughly surfaced limestone splinter is a black-outlined figure, the work of an artist of the end of the 18th dynasty, representing a young woman, in profile, in one of the movements of a dance. Lightly she touches the ground with toes and finger tips, her slender body curved gracefully back, while the rich plaits of her black hair fall to the ground.

The annular ear-ring in the lobe of her left ear is not represented as swinging earthward in conformity with the back-thrown movement of her head.

The dancer wears no ornaments on wrists or ankles. Around her hips is tied a black garment, decorated with woven three bands in a geometrical pattern.

PLATE LV

BOWL

(DYNASTY XVIII)

*Pottery bowl, lined with turquoise enamel. Diameter 6 ¹/₂ in.; height 2 in.
Drovetti collection. Catalogue no. 3368*

The bowl, in an excellent state of preservation, is covered in turquoise enamel. The inner surface is decorated with two short columns or supports, along one of the diameters, ending in two full-face heads of the goddess Hathor. Arranged symmetrically at both ends of a perpendicular diameter are three lotus flowers and two lotus buds.

Each head of the goddess is adorned with large eyes, of which the eyebrows form a single line with the nose. The mouth is blocked in by a rough stroke.

The wig of the goddess descends on either side of her neck in two locks which then curl upward, in the traditional style of the goddess.

The decoration in thinned-out black pigment, with masterly brush strokes, rapid and fluent, is typical of the end of the 18th dynasty.

PLATE LVI

Detail of Plate LV

DYNASTY XIX

PLATE LVII

STATUE OF RAMESSES II

(THIRD KING OF DYNASTY XIX, 1290-1224 B.C.)

Black granite statue. Total height 6 ft. 4 ³/₈ in.; height of face from chin to lower border of the " ḫprs̆ " 6 ¹¹/₁₆ in.;
width of face from ear to ear 7 ¹/₂ in. Drovetti collection. Catalogue no. 1380

Ever since Jean-François Champollion referred enthusiastically to his statue in his *Première lettre à M. le Duc de Blacas d'Aulps* (July 1824; p. 62 ff. of the Paris edition), it has been the best-known and most admired work in the Museum. It was discovered in 1818 by Jacques Rifaud, as the inscription he cut near the bottom of the right-hand side of the throne declares. It was brought to Turin in shapeless fragments and we owe its recomposition to the first curator of the Museum, Cav. Giulio Cordero di San Quintino.

Ramesses II is shown seated on a cubic throne with a low back, his body erect, his head bent slightly forward, the sculptor having perhaps noted this as being the king's natural posture. The face of the king, which in side view or profile is undamaged, must be acknowledged as a subtle portrait, showing austerity of expression tempered by serene majesty. Seen from the front, a view to be avoided by the visitor, the face of the king betrays a peculiar deformation: the nose, for example, which is described as *particulièrement mince*, no longer presents a clean line but appears considerably swollen at the end. The face of the king was sculptured to be enjoyed only from the side view, or in profile.

On his head Ramesses II is wearing the so-called blue helmet (in Egyptian *ḫprs̆*) with the uraeus in its customary position at the front. He is not wearing a ritual beard. Round his neck is a rich necklace. He is clothed in the official costume of his period, which consists chiefly in a thin pleated tunic with sleeves, over which is thrown another pleated garment covering his left shoulder, from which it falls to the left wrist.

In his right hand he holds the *ḥq* sceptre, in his left the stylized emblematic staff. On his shoulders are two cartouches bearing his name in vertical writing, above which are engraved two ostrich feathers. Another royal cartouche is visible in the centre of his belt. A vertical line of inscription runs down the front of his tunic. Two other lines of vertical inscription are to be found on the rear plinth.

The king's feet are shod in sandals, the wide soles of which rest on nine bows, engraved on the flat top of the base (see description of Plate XXII), symbolizing Egyptian supremacy over nine neighbouring peoples.

On the left side of the front of the throne the artist has sculptured a small figure of Nofretari, the first wife of the king (2 ft. ³/₄ in. high), and on the right the figure of his son Amen-her-khopechef (1 ft. 7 ³/₈ in. high), both dressed in the pleated garments of the time and extending respectively their right and left arms toward the legs of the sovereign.

Ernesto Schiaparelli discovered the tomb of Queen Nofretari in the Valley of the Queens in 1904. The scanty finds of funerary equipment obtained are displayed in a case in Exhibition Room III on the first floor, together with a small-scale model of the tomb.

It seems out of place here to enter into the question (raised from time to time, only to drop back into oblivion) of the attribution of this statue to Sety I, the father of Ramesses II; it has been claimed that Ramesses usurped or rather re-utilized his father's statue, having found it unfinished in the workshop of the royal sculptor. The arguments in support of this thesis are purely hypothetical and subjective, and a careful examination of the statue is all that is needed to refute them.

The text cut by J. Rifaud, mentioned above, is the following:

Dʳᵗ PAR J�pʳ
Rifaud AU SÈRVICE DE
Mʳ DROVETTi A thèbès Sᴿ.
1818

PLATE LVIII

Detail of Plate LVII

PLATE LIX

Detail of Plate LVII

PLATE LX

RAMESSES II
SEATED BETWEEN AMON-RA AND MUT, GODS OF THEBES
(DYNASTY XIX, 1290-1224 B.C.)

Triad hewn from a single block of red granite. The beard of Amon-Ra is missing, the remaining portions of the left arm of the goddess Mut, of which the hand is missing, have been restored. The front parts of the feet of both Ramesses II and Mut are damaged. Total height 5 ft. 8 ¹/₂ in., width 3 ft. 8 ¹/₈ in. Drovetti collection. Catalogue no. 767

Seated between the Theban deities Amon-Ra and Mut, both embracing him, sits Ramesses II, who in his turn embraces the god and goddess.

The king's face differs notably from the famous black granite statue reproduced in Plate LVII. The slightly curved twist of the mouth deserves attention. The goddess Mut is slender in form and is wearing anklets.

The intentions expressed so eloquently by the group are self-evident: in the first place there is the celebration and commemoration of the special favour and love of Amon-Ra and Mut which Ramesses II enjoys; in the second there is an open declaration of the divinity of the king, who occupies the place of the third member of the Theban triad, that of Khonsu, the son of Amon-Ra and Mut.

This group, which was greatly admired by the abbot Prof. Costanzo Gazzera in the early years of the last century, when he wrote of the Egyptian monuments in the Museum bearing the names of kings (*Monumenti egizi del Museo contenenti leggende reali*), seems too coldly academic for our taste today.

On the back of the rear wall against which the king and the Theban deities are resting, in the bottom right-hand corner, is cut the signature of J. Rifaud:

J · �q Rifaud
1818

PLATE LXII

STATUE BEARING THE NAME OF RAMESSES II
(SECOND INTERMEDIATE PERIOD)

Statue in quartziferous syenite. Mutilated, with damaged forehead, nose and royal head-dress. The legs are broken off at the knees and the lower part of the right leg and the left foot are missing. Height 7 ft. 4 ¹/₄ in. Drovetti collection. Catalogue no. 1381

The statue stands upright, with the left foot forward. The arms hang down and the open palms rest on the fold of a linen garment, closely pleated, which falls in front in a wide triangle. The king, whose trunk is naked, is distinguishable by the typical linen head-dress or *nemes*, with a uraeus at the front, and by the ritual beard on his chin. On the belt of his garment can be read the king's name, Ramesses, enclosed in a cartouche, which we can translate " The god Ra generated him, beloved of Amon ". In the vertical line of text in the (metal) decoration terminating at the bottom in two uraei, is the so-called praenomen engraved in two cartouches, preceded by the group *n.i śu.t bi.ti*, generally translated as " King of southern Egypt and northern Egypt, " and the name, preceded by the group *śʒ rʿ* = " son of the god Ra. " The common apposition *nb tʒ.ui* = " lord of the two territories " (southern and northern Egypt) forms part of the prae-nomen, while the apposition *nb hʒ.u* = " lord of crowns " forms part of the nomen (Plate LXIII).

The view of the figure's left side, on the flat surface at the side of the leg, reveals distinctly a female figure, engraved with studied care, but mutilated by the loss of the lower portion. This figure represents the queen; she is engraved in left profile, distinguished by a remarkably long neck and holding her right arm half-raised in an act of homage, while her left arm hangs down by her side. On her head she is wearing the solar disk and two long ostrich plumes, erect on the sacred image of a hawk goddess, whose wings droop open behind the ears of the queen. At the side her name was inscribed: undoubtedly it was the sculptor's intention to represent Nofretari, the first wife of Ramesses II. Today all that remains of the inscription is the introductory title: *ḥm.t n.i śu.t* = " wife of king... " (Plate LXIV). On the flat surface at the other side is cut the group *n.i śu.t bi.ti*: the royal praenomen which should have followed has been erased.

It is evident that the features of the statue in question fail completely to reproduce or even to recall those of Ramesses II. The deep-set eyes, the heavy lids, the protuberant straight-cut lips are nowhere to be found in portraits of the 19th dynasty. The name of Ramesses legible on the royal garment need not mislead us: it was added at a later date after the original royal name had been erased. That this is the case is proved by the slightly sunken surface of the portion of the belt on which the name of Ramesses is visible.

As the characteristics of 18th dynasty sculpture are likewise entirely lacking in this statue, it seems obvious to attribute it to the Second Intermediate Period, to which, as Jacques Vandier has justly pointed out, are assignable a number of royal statues of a certain value, vigorously sculptured and harmoniously proportioned.

PLATE LXI

Detail of Plate LX

PLATE LXI

Detail of Plate LX

PLATE LXII

STATUE BEARING THE NAME OF RAMESSES II
(SECOND INTERMEDIATE PERIOD)

Statue in quartziferous syenite. Mutilated, with damaged forehead, nose and royal head-dress. The legs are broken off at the knees and the lower part of the right leg and the left foot are missing. Height 7 ft. 4 ¹/₄ in. Drovetti collection. Catalogue no. 1381

The statue stands upright, with the left foot forward. The arms hang down and the open palms rest on the fold of a linen garment, closely pleated, which falls in front in a wide triangle. The king, whose trunk is naked, is distinguishable by the typical linen head-dress or *nemes*, with a uraeus at the front, and by the ritual beard on his chin. On the belt of his garment can be read the king's name, Ramesses, enclosed in a cartouche, which we can translate "The god Ra generated him, beloved of Amon". In the vertical line of text in the (metal) decoration terminating at the bottom in two uraei, is the so-called praenomen engraved in two cartouches, preceded by the group *n.i śu.t bi.ti*, generally translated as "King of southern Egypt and northern Egypt," and the name, preceded by the group *śʼ rʻ* = "son of the god Ra." The common apposition *nb tʼ.ui* = "lord of the two territories" (southern and northern Egypt) forms part of the prae-nomen, while the apposition *nb ḥʼu* = "lord of crowns" forms part of the nomen (Plate LXIII).

The view of the figure's left side, on the flat surface at the side of the leg, reveals distinctly a female figure, engraved with studied care, but mutilated by the loss of the lower portion. This figure represents the queen; she is engraved in left profile, distinguished by a remarkably long neck and holding her right arm half-raised in an act of homage, while her left arm hangs down by her side. On her head she is wearing the solar disk and two long ostrich plumes, erect on the sacred image of a hawk goddess, whose wings droop open behind the ears of the queen. At the side her name was inscribed: undoubtedly it was the sculptor's intention to represent Nofretari, the first wife of Ramesses II. Today all that remains of the inscription is the introductory title: *ḥm.t n.i śu.t* = "wife of king..." (Plate LXIV). On the flat surface at the other side is cut the group *n.i śu.t bi.ti*: the royal praenomen which should have followed has been erased.

It is evident that the features of the statue in question fail completely to reproduce or even to recall those of Ramesses II. The deep-set eyes, the heavy lids, the protuberant straight-cut lips are nowhere to be found in portraits of the 19th dynasty. The name of Ramesses legible on the royal garment need not mislead us: it was added at a later date after the original royal name had been erased. That this is the case is proved by the slightly sunken surface of the portion of the belt on which the name of Ramesses is visible.

As the characteristics of 18th dynasty sculpture are likewise entirely lacking in this statue, it seems obvious to attribute it to the Second Inter-mediate Period, to which, as Jacques Vandier has justly pointed out, are assignable a number of royal statues of a certain value, vigorously sculptured and harmoniously proportioned.

PLATE LXIII

Detail of Plate LXII

PLATE LXIV

View of the left side of the statue in Plate LXII

PLATE LXIV

Plate LXV

ENGRAVING OF A ROYAL HEAD
(DYNASTY XIX)

Engraved on limestone, the head is damaged by a chip at the top left-hand corner, so that part of the wig and the head of the uraeus are missing. Height of fragment 1 ft. $^1/_4$ in., width at widest point 9 $^1/_2$ in. Drovetti collection. Catalogue no. 7051

In left profile, the chief characteristic of the royal head is the heavy wig with cylindrical plaits, sculptured with finished artistry and extreme attention to minutiae. Set high over the forehead a diadem encircles his head, fastening at the back; entwined with it is a uraeus of which the head, now missing, originally reared over the regal brows.

Another uraeus is visible hanging down on the extreme left of the diadem.

A stylized beard, widening at the end, completes the face, which is recognizable as that of Sety I, of the 19th dynasty, an identification made possible by certain characteristic features: his aquiline nose, and his small lips turning down at the corners.

PLATE LXVI

ROYAL PAPYRUS: COLUMNS III, IV, V
(DYNASTY XIX)

Papyrus inscribed on both sides. Height of fragments, in their present lay-out, about 1 ft. 4 ¹/₈ in. Length 6 ft.
Drovetti collection. Catalogue no. 1874

The fragments of the *Royal Papyrus* (known also as the *Turin King List* and the *Royal Canon*) are displayed framed under glass in Exhibition Room VI, on the first floor. In its original state the *Papyrus* consisted of many columns, of which we have the remnants of eleven, all damaged and incomplete. These listed the kings who governed Egypt from the time of the first divine and mythological dynasties down to the 19th historical dynasty. In its present state the eleventh remaining column lists the names of kings attributed to the 17th Manethan dynasty.

The hieratic text, the work of a scribe of the 19th dynasty, was written on the back or secondary side of the roll of papyrus after the main side or front had been filled with eight columns, in cursive writing, of accounts of the taxes due in kind from Libyan oases and paid into the Treasury during the reign of Ramesses II.

It is still rumoured that the *Papyrus* was found intact by Drovetti. Be that as it may, it reached Turin in " minute fragments " intermixed with many other bits of the numerous papyri of the Drovetti collection. The first to work on them was J.-F. Champollion, who made good progress in separating and distinguishing them during his stay in Turin in 1824 and 1825. The work begun by Champollion was continued and improved upon by the German scholar Gustav Seyffarth who, in order better to connect the separate fragments, wisely followed the clues offered by variations in the papyrus fibres employed.

The name of the first of the historical kings, Menes, can be read in the second column, on lines 10 and 11. His successors were listed one after the other, from column to column, in groups of varying numbers, with mention at the side of the length of each reign in years, months and days. A sum drawn up after the last name in each group gave the number of the members and the total of the years during which they reigned.

The division of the kings into thirty dynasties dates back to Manetho, an Egyptian priest who lived during the reigns of Ptolemy I and Ptolemy II, and who may have had access to sources and documents unknown to us today. The Manethan tables are in utter contradiction of the data in this papyrus with respect to the number of the dynasties, the spelling of the kings' names, the number of kings in each dynasty and the length of their reigns.

This plate reproduces columns III, IV and V, from right to left. In line 5 of column III the name of Zoser (*Dśr*) can be read, a king of the 3rd Manethan dynasty, buried in his own monumental burial place: the step pyramid at Saqqara. If the remaining portion of this column had been preserved entire, we could have read there the names of famous kings of the 4th and 5th dynasties. On the twenty-fifth line we can read the name of Unas ("Ovvoς) who, according to Manetho, was the last sovereign of the 5th dynasty. On the next line, the sum of the years relating to this group of kings has been lost through damage to the papyrus.

Column IV, down to lines 16 and 17, lists the names of kings who in the *Papyrus* form another group. On line 8 we read the name of Nitocris (Νίτωκρις), the queen who, according to Manetho, was the last to reign in the 6th dynasty. Lines 16-17, although damaged, provide the valuable information that from the reign of Menes down to the last member of this group, a period of 955 years and 10 days elapsed. Continuing down to line 26 of this column IV, and on to the tenth line of column V, we have the names of eighteen kings, which the *Papyrus* unites in a further and separate group. From the eleventh to the seventeenth line are listed the names of six further kings, the same number as Manetho ascribes to his 11th dynasty.

From line 19 to 25 a new group is introduced, connected with the town of Ith-tawe, south of Memphis. The names we read are those of the first six of the eight kings who form Manetho's 12th dynasty.

Altogether this fragmentary and mutilated text of the surviving columns III-V carried the names and dates of kings which Manetho divided into no less than ten dynasties, from the 3rd to the 12th: in this lies the importance of the portion of the *Royal Papyrus* reproduced here.

PLATE LXVII

HUSBAND AND WIFE
(DYNASTY XIX)

Limestone group.   Height 2 ft. 7 ¹/₂ in.
From the excavations of Ernesto Schiaparelli at Der el-Medina, 1905.   Catalogue supplement no. 6127

On the left of the group, on a high-backed seat, sits the husband Pentèwew, who during his life held office as a " servant in the Place of Truth " (see description of Plate XXI); on his right sits Neftere, his wife: both wear the linen garments of the 19th dynasty, and wigs of the same period cover their heads. Five of their children, together with their names, are engraved on the surface at the back of the seat; the figures of ten more are engraved with their names on the left and right ends of the seat. The figure of another daughter is visible cut into the back of the seat, in the space between husband and wife.

PLATE LXVIII

PENMERN'EB WITH THE RAM-HEADED IMAGE OF AMON-RA
(DYNASTY XIX)

Limestone statue. Height 2 ft. 1 ¹/₄ in. Drovetti collection. Catalogue no. 3032

The figure of Penmern'eb, " servant in the Place of Truth, " a title and office which are explained in the description of Plate XXI, rests back on his heels. Between his knees he holds a rectangular pedestal supporting the ram's head of the god to whose service he was expressly dedicated: a large-scale head of Amon-Ra, god of Thebes, with a beard on the chin.

Penmern'eb is wearing a closely pleated linen garment, from waist to heels. He wears a short beard on his chin and bracelets on his wrists.

On his right shoulder is lightly engraved the iconographic figure of Amon-Ra of Thebes; on his left the figure of a queen of the 18th dynasty, Ahmes-Nofretari, according to the name in the cartouche; on the back is engraved the iconographic figure of Hathor.

PLATE LXIX

Detail of Plate LXVIII

PLATE LXX

INR, GUARDIAN OF THE TEMPLE
OF THE GODDESS HATHOR IN KOS
(NEW KINGDOM)

Black granite statuette.   Height 1 ft. 2 ⁷/₈ in.   Drovetti collection.   Catalogue no. 3018

The figure is represented in a kneeling posture, resting back on his heels. The statuette is well preserved except for the right arm, damaged from the elbow down, and the rectangular base of which the front portion is missing, and some slight scratches besides.

In life Inr held a single office, as recorded on the one line of text on the plinth at the back of the statue: the office of *s̓u* or guardian, presumably of the temple of the goddess Hathor in Kos, the capital city of the 14th nome or district in southern Egypt, the Roman Cusae, and modern Al-Kusîyah, mentioned on the same plinth.

Of stocky build, his stoutness has been crudely portrayed by the sculptor: the fat limbs and shoulders, the short bull-like neck.

The form of the face, fashioned in a long oval—the soft fleshy cheeks, the high forehead, the eyes close to the surface—produces the impression of certain individual characteristics of a subject which the sculptor has endeavoured to immortalize in stone. The figure is not wearing on his head the stylized wig of the period: it has been sculptured realistically as bald, the surviving hair ringed round like a crown ending at the temples, a style implying old age, as we know from certain rare and delightful extemporized sketches on ostracons (see ostracon no. 2324, from the French expeditions of Der el-Medîna, published by J. Vandier d'Abbadie), and on papyri (see catalogue no. 2031 of the Turin Egyptian Museum).

He is wearing a thin tunic, of which the sculptor has shown the short pleated sleeves, and from his waist down to his ankles, a garment of heavy linen, closely pleated. On the front are added puffed-out pleats opening like a fan, such as are to be found on both statues and stelae of the New Kingdom from the 18th dynasty on, as accessories of male dress.

The left hand of the figure holds a short, possibly wooden, handle which supports the stylized image of the goddess Hathor, whose name and title " Lady of Kos " are lightly engraved on the handle. The right hand, passing under his chin, rests on the top of the image. As the right arm is damaged from the elbow down it is impossible to determine with certainty the exact position of the right hand; but the remnant leads us to suppose that it must have rested, palm open, on the image of the goddess.

This interesting statuette of Inr can be attributed to a provincial sculptor of the 19th dynasty, at the latest.

PLATE LXXI

A YOUNG WOMAN
(DYNASTY XIX)

Wooden statuette. The right-hand side of the wig is damaged; the right arm and both feet are missing; the original base on which the statue stood has been lost. Height 1 ft. 3 ³/₈ in.
Drovetti collection. Catalogue no. 3105

This is the most graceful of the female figures in the possession of the Museum. The deceased, sculptured standing with the left foot forward in the usual posture, is wearing a linen robe reaching almost to the ground; one end of the robe is wrapped closely around her so as to cover her left arm, which is folded across her breast. The heavy black plaits of the wig, adorned with a floral decoration at the top, fall low over her breasts and behind her shoulders. Around her neck she is wearing a precious necklace.

The spiritual character of this figure, portrayed in her fullest beauty, has been caught and immortalized in her attitude and in the expression of her highly sensitive face. Slim in form, with long lower limbs, accentuated in the back view (see Plate LXXXII), the folds of her robe, carefully arranged, seem to give her a touch of ineffable lightness.

As the original wooden base of the statuette has been lost, we shall never know the name of this young woman. It is unfortunate too that we have no means of learning the name of the sculptor, the creator of this masterpiece. His work will unquestionably be a source of constant admiration for all who visit the Egyptian Museum in Turin, whether from Italy or abroad.

PLATE LXXII

Back view of the statuette in Plate LXXI

PLATE LXXII

Back view of the statuette in Plate LXXI

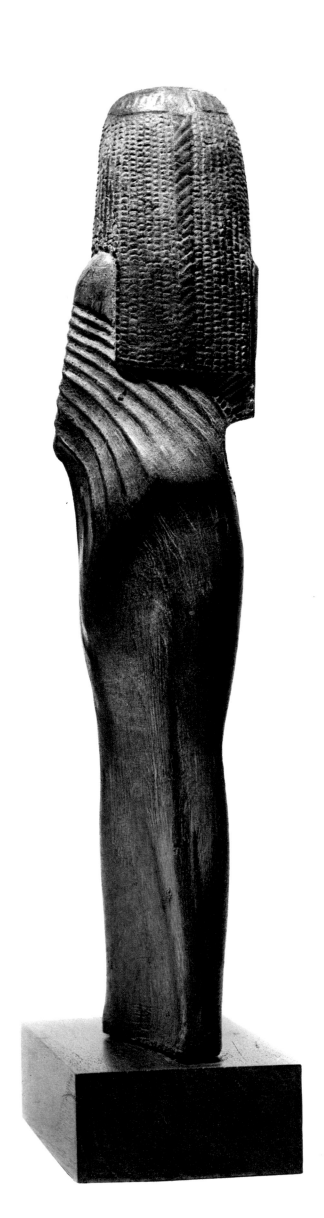

PLATE LXXIII

STATUETTE OF A BEARER OF A SACRED EMBLEM
(DYNASTY XIX)

Wooden statuette.   Height 1 ft. 5 in.   Drovetti collection.   Catalogue no. 3049

This standing figure was sculptured with the left foot forward, in one of the most usual postures. He is wearing a closely pleated linen kilt; over this is knotted around the waist a tightly pleated shawl or *sari*, which enwraps the hips and of which a strip, likewise closely pleated, falls down the front, opening out in the form of a triangle.

The left hand of the figure presses closely to his side an uninscribed cylindrical pole, on the top of which is the head of a falcon. The right hand, which hangs down along the right side, is clenched into a fist.

The loss of the original base, and of the text which was usually inscribed there, has deprived us of data which would have been valuable for more reasons than one: it is therefore impossible for us to give a name to this figure.

PLATE LXXIV

BEARER OF TWO SACRED IMAGES
(DYNASTY XIX)

Wooden statuette. Height 1 ft. 11 ⁵/₈ in.; length of original base 1 ft. 1 in., width 5 ⁵/₈ in., height 2 ³/₄ in. Drovetti collection. Catalogue no. 3048

Penbuy, the figure portrayed, was engaged in work in the " Place of Truth " (= Theban necropolis). He stands before us erect, with his left foot forward. He presses to his sides two long, cylindrical poles on the top of which are statuettes of the gods Amon-Ra (considerably damaged) and Ptah, both on thrones.

Penbuy is wearing a pleated linen garment, from his waist to a little below his knees. Over this is worn a closely pleated shawl or *sari*, like the one worn by the figure in Plate LXXIII. His face is framed in the elaborate plaits of his hair, which fall symmetrically along the sides of his cheeks, down to his breast.

The vertical line of text, inscribed on the strip of the shawl down the front of the linen garment, expresses the wish that everything left on the table of offerings of the Theban god Amon-Ra should be placed before the deceased.

On the right face of the supporting plinth, cut in low relief by the hand of a master, is the figure of the wife (Plate LXXV). Standing in left profile, she is wearing a long full garment; on her head is a wig surmounted by a diadem, with a lotus flower over her brows, and a pomade cone on the top of her head. Her right hand holds a lotus flower and lotus buds, their stems twisted around her hand. She fills the office of " great singer of the goddess Mut, the lady of Išr.w. " (1)

(1) The name given to the temple and sacred lake of the goddess, near the modern Karnak, from the time of the 18th dynasty onward. In this temple were found two statues of the goddess Sachmis, seated on a throne and standing, which today are shown in two of the Museum's sculpture rooms.

PLATE LXXV

Detail of Plate LXXIV

Plate LXXVI

A HIGH PRIEST OF PTAH, GOD OF MEMPHIS
(NEW KINGDOM)

Stone funerary statuette. Height 7 ¹/₄ in. Drovetti collection. Catalogue no. 2666

The deceased, sculptured in a standing position, bore the name of Neb-mehit (*nb mḥi.t*), and in life filled the extremely high office of " High priest of Ptah, god of Memphis " and the further office of " Chief Director of Works. " He is represented in his official garb, a linen robe with sleeves, reaching down to his ankles. Over this robe he is wearing a shawl tied around his waist, such as was worn by other figures of the New Kingdom (see Plates LXXIII and LXXIV), a strip of which, fanning out into a triangle, falls down the front of his robe in wide pleats.

The vertical inscription down the front of this shawl gives the name of the official and of the positions he occupied. On his head he is wearing an unusual wig, one lock of which falls down in a curl on the right. His feet are bare; on his chin is a short square beard.

The side and back views of the statuette, a *shawabti* figure (*š꞉w꞉ b.ti > š꞉b.ti*) later known as *ushabti* (*ušb.ti*), carry on four horizontal lines passages from Chapter VI of the so-called " Book of the Dead "; these it was believed would enable the statuette to take the place of the deceased, at his explicit request, in the execution of tasks imposed on him in the Other World.

PLATE LXXVII

NAOS

(DYNASTY XIX)

Wooden naos, the sides decorated on the exterior with polychromatic scenes. Height 1 ft. 1 in., length of sides 1 ft. 1 1/16 in., width 5 9/16 in.
Drovetti collection. Catalogue no. 2446

The small wooden naos, or shrine, is dedicated to the triad of the First Cataract, near Elephantine, a triad comprising the god Khnum and the goddesses Satis and Anukis, by Kasa (*kꜣ-sꜣ*), one of the " servants in the Place of Truth " (see Plate XXI), who lived under the reign of Ramesses II in the 19th dynasty. A limestone stela of Kasa belongs to the Bankes collection (at Kingston Lacy, near Wimborne, Dorset) on which he is represented together with many of his relatives.

The naos, highly interesting in that it was the first, and for many years the only exemplar discovered in Egypt, rests on a flat rectangular base shaped like a sledge. In front of the double door, with knobs on the outside so that it can be closed with a cord, there is a narrow porch with two cylindrical columns each bearing a single vertical line of hieroglyphic inscription, the one on the right dedicated to the god Khnum, the one on the left to the goddess Anukis. The two columns, topped with capitals forming two-faced heads of the goddess Hathor, support a projecting cornice.

The surface of the exterior wall on the left is divided horizontally into two halves. The upper section contains a scene of the goddess Anukis sailing on sacred water in a boat with helms, decorated both at prow and stern by a protome of Hathor, the goddess being recognizable by her head-dress of cow's horns with the solar disk between them. Anukis is seated on a cubic throne with a low back, under a small canopy surmounted by uraei with yellow solar disks upon their heads. On her head is the traditional feather head-dress, with alternate red and deep green feathers. She is wearing a light green dress with straps over the shoulders. In her right hand she is holding the *ꜥnḫ* amulet and in her left the *wꜣs* sceptre. In front of the goddess stands a one-legged table supporting a vase with a large lotus flower. The white wall at the back of the canopy sets off the figure of the goddess in relief (Plate LXXVIII).

The other half of the wall is subdivided horizontally into two smaller sections. The first, connected to the upper half by the branch which flows from the sacred water on which Anukis' boat is moving, is crossed on the right by a boat with helm, rowed by four oarsmen, relatives of Kasa. On the left are reproduced Kasa himself and one of his sons, intent on the purification and presentation of offerings. In the section below six figures, seen kneeling in left profile, are wearing white linen garments, and are engaged in paying homage to the goddess and presenting offerings: they are Kasa, his wife, his two daughters and two sons.

The exterior wall on the other side is divided horizontally into two equal halves. In the upper section Kasa is recognizable on the left, engaged in presenting offerings to the triad of the First Cataract. In the lower section, in right profile, are a row of Kasa's relatives, each with offerings to the gods in his hands.

The outside of the rear wall is covered with six vertical lines of inscription containing a prayer to Anukis for the grace of a good burial in the western necropolis of Thebes, and other prayers to the remaining gods of the triad.

The interior walls of the naos are bare. On the back wall is a small shelf, only a few centimetres above the base, to hold the images of the gods of the triad.

Clearly the goddess Anukis enjoyed first place in Kasa's religious observances and worship. Two further inscriptions, written in four vertical lines on each panel of the door, are both addressed to her.

PLATE LXXVIII

Side view of the naos in Plate LXXVII

Plate LXXIX

STELA OF IPY

(DYNASTY XIX)

Limestone stela. Height 1 ft. 10 ¹/₂ in., width 1 ft. 3 in. Drovetti collection. Catalogue no. 7357

The stela, with arched top, shows no traces of paint. The surface, divided horizontally into two unequal parts, is covered with scenes executed by two different sculptural techniques—the one in bas-relief, while the principal characteristic of the other is that the figures are executed in sunk relief.

The top section shows four deities facing each other in two groups: in the centre left is Osiris, on a low pedestal, wearing the *ȝtfu* crown and holding the *ḥqȝ* sceptre and a flagellum, while on his right stands Hathor, recognizable by her traditional head-dress, presented here in her function as funerary goddess "at the head of the western necropolis of Thebes." In profile facing Osiris stands Ra-Horakhte, falcon-headed, with the *wȝs* sceptre in his right hand, and holding the *'nḫ* amulet in his left, "the great god who resides on the western mountain Mȝnw;" and on his left king Amenhotep I, of the 18th dynasty, "the good god" whom we know to have been deified after death together with his mother (see Plate XXI). His wig resembles the one which adorns the head of the king in the relief reproduced in Plate LXV. His wide, closely pleated robe reaches down to his ankles. In his right hand he grasps the *ḥqȝ* sceptre and a flagellum and, in his left which hangs down by his side, the *'nḫ* amulet.

On the left of the lower section, on a wide high-backed wooden chair, sits Ipy, who during his life held office as "servant in the Place of Truth," with his wife by his side. Near the seat stands a naked child, one of his sons. At the other side of a four-legged wooden table laden with food (see Plate LXXX), stand two adult sons and a daughter. The first of these, wearing a leopard skin, is shown in the ritual act of sprinkling the offerings; the second bears an offering in his right hand. Their sister, who is less tall than her brothers, is holding the wings of a fowl in her right hand, and a lotus flower in her left.

This stela is one of the most valuable of those of the New Kingdom, for the fine artistry with which all the figures, whether gods or mortals, are carved, and for the harmoniously balanced distribution of these figures in the two sections. At first the eye fails to notice the disproportion in the representation of the deceased and his wife who, although seated, are the same height as the standing figures of their sons.

The Abbot Gazzera wrote over a century ago that this stela filled him with pleasure and wonder every time he set out to examine it: an aesthetic judgement and evaluation which we can still share with him today.

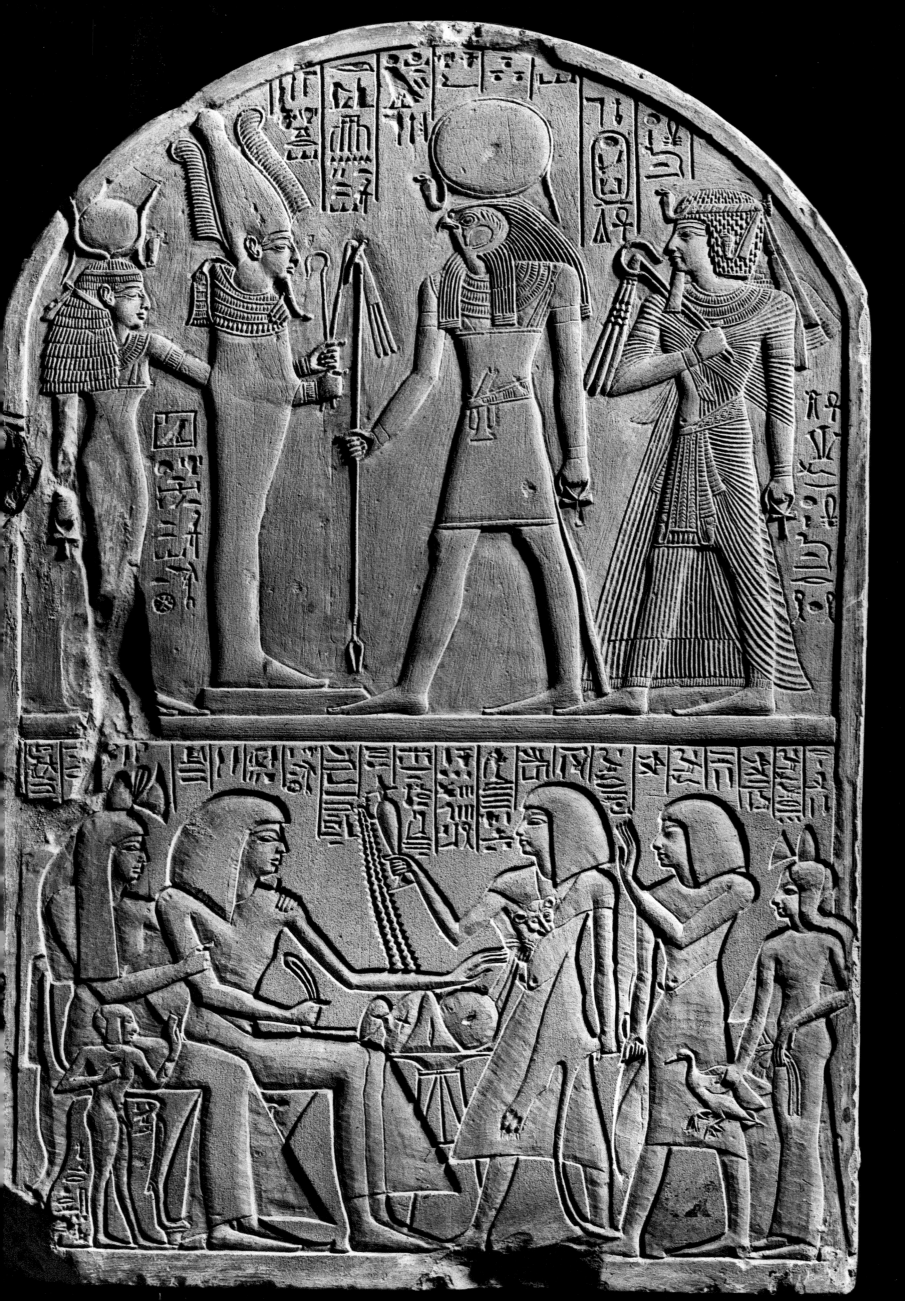

Plate LXXX

Detail of Plate LXXIX

PLATE LXXXI

RECTANGULAR LID OF A LADY'S TOILET BOX
(DYNASTY XVIII-XIX)

Wooden lid.   Length 5 ⁷/₈ in., width 2 ¹/₂ in.   Drovetti collection.   Catalogue no. 6416

The scene portrayed fills roughly a third of the top of the lid. The rest of the space above and below is filled in with an identical pattern.

A gazelle running toward the right has been overtaken and ferociously attacked by two dogs. One of them has leapt onto his back and seized the gazelle's muzzle in its jaws.

It is interesting to note that the two dogs, although shown respectively in left and right profile, are almost identical.

PLATE LXXXII

TOILET SPOON
(DYNASTY XVIII-XIX)

Wooden toilet spoon, in a poor state of preservation. Length 10 ¹/₄ in. Drovetti collection. Catalogue no. 6442

Among the few women's toilet articles of the New Kingdom housed in the Museum, we have thought this cosmetic spoon deserving of a place among the plates reproduced in the present volume, even though it is in a poor state of preservation.

Fashioned from a single piece of light-weight wood, its handle originally consisted of two pairs of lotus flowers and their stems, in open work, on either side of a bunch of papyrus flowers piled up into a floral column, crowned by a lotus flower. The top of the spoon is a concave bowl into which cosmetics were measured; oval in shape, it rests on horizontally placed bunches of flowers. Together, the handle and bowl of the spoon cannot fail to call to mind, even if they do not actually reproduce it, the well-known form of the ʿnḫ amulet (♀): the unknown artist who fashioned this object bore in mind its propitious influence over the woman who was to hold the spoon between her fingers.

A number of museums abroad (Cairo, Berlin, the British Museum in London and the Louvre in Paris) can boast of numerous wooden toilet spoons, valuable for their excellent state of preservation. In spite of the fragility of the material in which they were fashioned, they bear witness, as well or better than anything else, to the variety of forms and subjects, the refinement and wealth of fantasy, lavished by the Egyptians on their " minor arts. "

Plate LXXXIII

SKETCH ON OSTRACON
(DYNASTY XIX)

Limestone ostrakon. Height 5 $^7/_8$ in., width 6 $^1/_4$ in.
From the excavations of Ernesto Schiaparelli at Bibân el-Ḥarīm (Valley of the Queens), 1903–1905.
Catalogue supplement no. 5690

The surface of the fragment of limestone, irregular in form, is covered with part of a female figure, in right profile, sketched in black with firm strokes.

PLATE LXXXIV

SKETCH ON OSTRACON
(DYNASTY XIX)

Limestone ostrakon. Height 9 ¹/₂ in., width 6 ¹/₂ in.
From the excavations of Ernesto Schiaparelli at Bibân el-Ḥarîm (Valley of the Queens), 1903-1905.
Catalogue supplement no. 5689

On the surface of the limestone fragment, irregular in outline and only partially smooth, is an extemporized sketch in black brush-strokes traced by a firm hand, showing a female figure in right profile, incomplete because headless and with the lower portions of the legs missing.

A transparent robe has been suggested by strokes in fainter black.

DYNASTY XX

PLATE LXXXV

KING WITH PRISONER

(DYNASTY XX, 1184-1087 B.C.)

Sandstone group, with traces of paint (the eyes of the king, painted black), on original base.
Uninscribed.   Height 1 ft. 11 in.   Drovetti collection.   Catalogue no. 1392

The king, who cannot be identified with any certainty owing to the lack of unequivocal iconographic details, is standing with his left foot forward, and wearing the crown *atef*, on which are two horizontal ram's horns ending in two uraei, only one of which (that on the left horn) now remains. Another uraeus, now missing, was originally placed over his brows.

The front braids of his wig fall to his breast. His chin is beardless and he is barefoot. He is wearing the *scentō* or linen kilt; from its belt must originally have hung the rich ornament characterizing the royal costume of the New Kingdom, invisible today owing to the damaged state of the statuette but in the past it must have been picked out and finished in colour. In his right hand, carried at the height of his breast, the king is holding the handle of a square-headed axe; in his left hand, down by his side, he is grasping the hair of a prisoner so as to force him to raise his head. The prisoner is recognizably a Negro by his physical features: prominent fleshy lips and flat nose. His arms are tied behind his back and he is bent double, with the teeth of the king's lion sunk in his belly.

This is one of the few groups which recall successful royal campaigns, portraying the traditional representation of a sovereign victorious over the enemies of Egypt.

Plate LXXXVI

THE GODDESS SACHMIS

(DYNASTY XX, 1151-1145 B.C.)

Black diorite statue, undamaged. Height 7 ft. 6 ¹/₂ in. Drovetti collection. Catalogue no. 270

The lion-headed goddess Sachmis, wife of the god Ptah of Memphis, was known as an evil deity with a malign influence: the bringer of sickness upon the people of Egypt and of suffering into their land.

The kings loved to compare themselves to Sachmis when, throwing themselves furiously into the heat of the battle, they put to flight foreign enemies banded together against Egypt.

The statue reproduced in this plate is one of the ten statues which represents the seated goddess in the possession of the Museum; eleven others, on a smaller scale, portray her standing, with the papyrus sceptre and the 'nḫ amulet in her hands. She is characterized by the solar disk with uraeus on her head. A rich necklace encircles her neck and falls over her breast. Her clenched left hand grasps the 'nḫ amulet. Her feet are bare.

On the front and sides of the throne are cartouches legibly engraved with the name of Ramesses IV of the 20th dynasty (1151-1145 B.C.).

On the top right-hand side is an inscription recording the discovery of the statue by Rifaud:

Dᵗ ᴘᴀʀ Jᵈ Rifᴀud

sculptᴇuʀ ᴀ thèbᴇs

ᴀu sèviᴄᴇ ᴅᴱ Mʳ Dʀovètti

Plate LXXXVII

TOMB OF RAMESSES IV

(THIRD KING OF DYNASTY XX, 1151-1145 B.C.)

Plan drawn up on a papyrus written on both sides; the initial portion on the right and the whole lower
portion are missing. Measurements of papyrus in its present state: height 1 ft. ¹/₄ in., length 3 ft. 5 ¹/₄ in.;
some fragments besides of which the exact position is uncertain.
Drovetti collection. Catalogue no. 1885

The reign of Ramesses IV, 1151-1145 B.C., was a short one. His tomb can be seen in the Valley of the Kings (Bibân el-Molûk), in the Theban necropolis on the western bank of the Nile.

The plan of this tomb, drawn by an unknown architect of the period, has reached us on the front of the Turin papyrus, written on both sides, but incomplete. The missing parts are about 2 feet on the right top of plate and a section 5 ¹/₂ inches high along the bottom right of plate.

The tomb consists of a series of chambers, most of which are rectangular in form, opening into one another in a line from right to left. A caption in hieratic cursive writing, in black ink, gives the measurements (length, breadth and height) of each chamber, and at times its name and purpose. For example, beginning at top of plate, the papyrus contains the end of a corridor or passage, followed by another rectangular chamber and the " Waiting room " (t̲w̲š̲ḥ. t iśq) which opens into the great " House of Gold " (pr n nbw) occupied by the monumental stone sarcophagus of the king. Leading out of this is another chamber, one section of which is named " seat of the *shawabti* funerary statuettes, " and a few smaller rooms defined as " treasuries. " The wooden doors of each of the rooms, fastened with bolts, are shown in the plan.

The whole tomb on the papyrus is enclosed with a wavy outline in reddish ink, blocked in with pink and filled up with oblique parallel lines of dots, alternately red and black, a conventional way of representing the hills into which the tomb was dug.

The measurements of the tomb are given in terms of the Egyptian unit of length, the " royal cubit " of seven palms or twenty-eight fingers (about 1 foot 8 ⁵/₈ inches). The architect did not calculate the measurements of the separate chambers in exact figures. According to the data furnished by the papyrus, the total length of the tomb of the king amounted to 160 royal cubits and 5 palms.

In the great " House of Gold " the architect showed the monumental pink granite sarcophagus surrounded by a number of vertical wooden walls. This sarcophagus, fashioned in the shape of a great cartouche, 10 feet 6 inches long, 6 feet 10 ⁵/₈ inches wide and 8 feet 2 ³/₈ inches high, has been preserved *in situ*. On its lid is the image of the king between the goddesses Isis and Nephthys.

On the back of the papyrus is a description of the royal tomb, in seven lines of cursive writing. The data given provide useful material for comparison with the actual tomb of Ramesses IV.

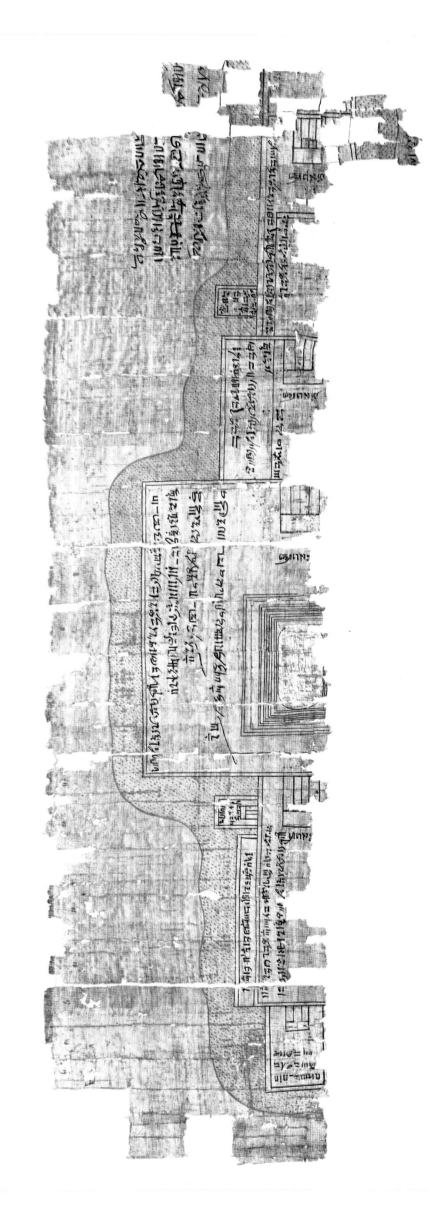

PLATE LXXXVIII

PAPYRUS OF THE GOLD MINES
AND THE SCHIST QUARRIES

(DYNASTY XX, ABOUT 1184-1087 B.C.)

Damaged papyrus, with portions missing. Length 9 ft. 3 in., height 1 ft. 4 ¹/₈ in.
Drovetti collection. Catalogue nos. 1879, 1899, 1969

This exceptionally important papyrus, the only example of ancient Egyptian map-drawing, is incomplete: both the beginning and end are missing and almost the whole is damaged by frequent gaps. The portion here reproduced is the least damaged, and is 2 feet 4 ¹/₈ inches long.

The pale pink area represents the mountainous zone of Wadi-Hammamat in which were located the gold deposits mined by the Egyptians, as we are told by the captions in minute cursive or hieratic writing which can be read here and there on the portions reproduced. In the top right-hand corner are visible the god Amon's whitish temple and houses for the workmen. Near the centre of the area is a whitish stela in the name of king Sety I of the 19th dynasty, and on the left of the stela a well, which is identifiable as the modern Bir el-Hammamat. Considerably below a rough road leads off toward the right: the map-maker has marked this with patches of colour to suggest the stones and rocks which made rough going of the route between the two chains of mountains, marked in black, leading to the quarries from which the Egyptians extracted the *bhni* stone (schist or basalt).

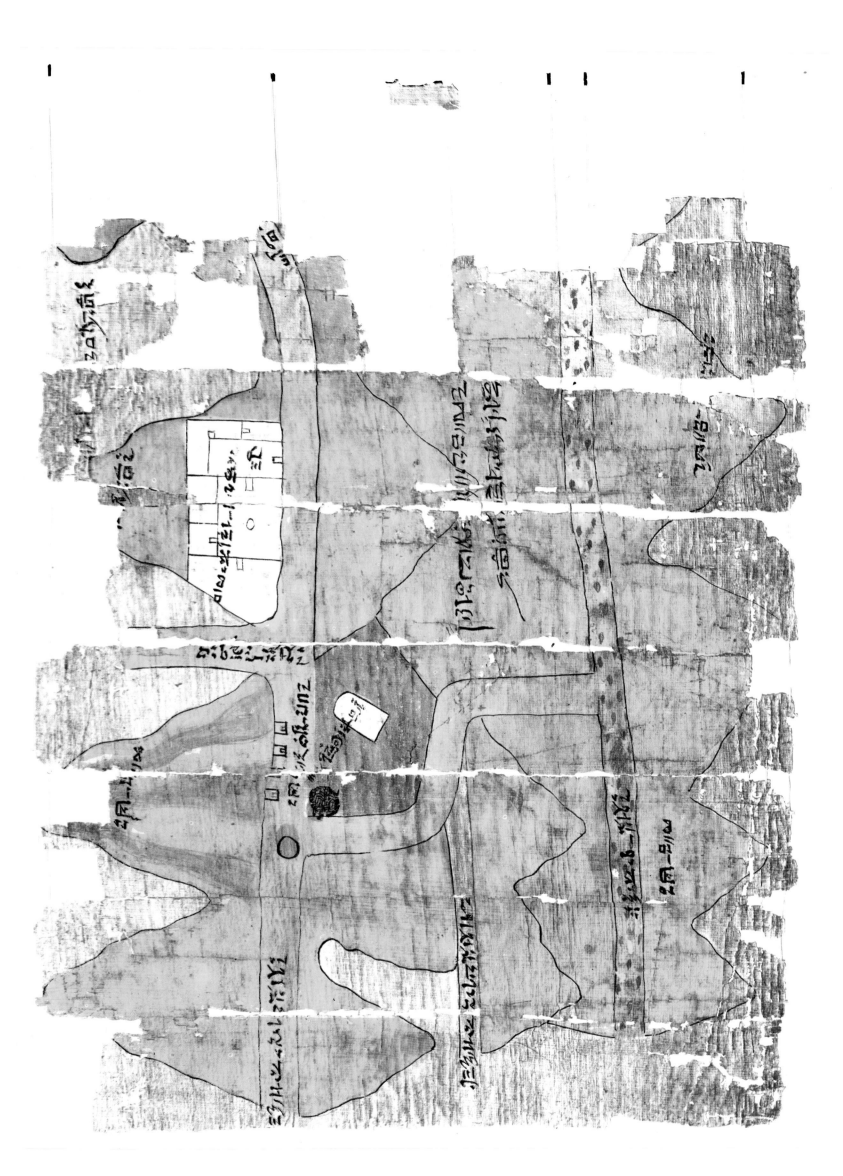

Plate LXXXIX

THE SONG OF THE SYCAMORE
(BEGINNING OF DYNASTY XX)

Papyrus. Height 1 ft. 3 ³/₈ in., length 2 ft. 1 ³/₈ in. Drovetti collection. Catalogue no. 1966

This Turin papyrus fragment, which can be attributed to the beginning of the 20th dynasty (about 1184 B.C.) on account of certain paleographic features, hands down to us two damaged pages of a literary text, of which the original length is unknown, in cursive or hieratic writing, reading from right to left. The first page, on the right, consists of fifteen horizontal lines of which the beginning is missing; the second, on the left, contains fourteen lines, and two in a smaller hand. Visible in the lines of text are the red punctuation marks common in the texts of the New Kingdom, probably intended to facilitate reading aloud.

The content of the first surviving page takes us to the heart of the story. Two short poetic compositions, in amorous vein, are offered in turn by the trees in a garden, pomegranate and fig, in celebration of the beauties of a young woman, the mistress of the garden, and of her loves. Longer than these is the passage which we have named the *Song of the Sycamore*. Full of touches of gentle irony and of details of the customs of Egyptian youth, we have thought fit to bring it to the knowledge of readers of today in a literal translation, following the lines as they were originally written. The *Song* begins with the last word of line 15 of page one, on the right, and continues through the fourteen lines of page two, to which is added the first word of line 15.

For a better understanding of the *Song*, we should add that it opens with the introduction of the protagonist, the sycamore tree, which the young mistress has planted with her own hands. We then learn of her plan: to indite a love letter inviting her lover (referred to in the text as *lover* and *brother*, in the same way as the young woman is called *sister*) to come to her in the garden to pass some time among friends, accompanied by his servants laden with provisions—bread, beer and fruit—and to spend there three days of happiness. When the two lovers, the mistress and her friend, walk apart from the group in the garden, the sycamore will keep silence as to what it hears and sees. With this declaration the *Song of the Sycamore* closes, after having seduced us through its images to dwell among the hopes and customs of nameless young Egyptian lovers some three thousand years ago.

The colour contrast between the red fruits and green leaves of the tree mentioned in the opening lines of the song is not uncommon in ancient oriental literary compositions. It can compare with the end of column V of Plate IX of the *Epopee of Gilgamesh* in Conteneau's well-known translation.

Page 1, line 15   *The small sycamore,*

Page 2, line 1   *which she has planted with her own hand, (when) it opens its mouth to speak the murmur of [its leaves is sweet as is]*

line 2   *the fragrance of honey. It is beautiful. Its graceful boughs are greener [than those of ...]*

line 3   *It is laden with ripe fruits, redder than the red jasper. Its leaves are*

line 4   *the colour of malachite. Its bark is the colour of green jasper. The ... are like*

line 5   *the tree " bšbš." It draws those who are not beneath it (because) its shadow freshens the air. It [gives] a letter of love into the hand*

line 6   *of a maiden, daughter of its chief gardener, and sends her running toward the loved one: " Come*

line 7   *and pass a moment among the young friends. The garden is in his day. Bower and tent are below me.*

line 8   *The men of the garden rejoice and are made glad when they see thee. Let the servants come*

line 9   *before me, furnished with their provisions. To run to thee is to be intoxicated without having drunk. " The servants*

line 10   *have come with provisions and have carried every kind of beer, every kind of bread; many flowers*

line 11   *of yesterday and today and every kind of fruit to eat.*
           Oh, may she pass the day happily,

line 12   *morning after morning, for three days, sitting in my shade.*
           Her friend is on her right hand. She

line 13   *gives him to drink and fulfils his commands.*
           While around them the drunkenness increases, she stays apart with her brother,

line 14   *walking beneath me, the sister, as she goes. (But) I will remain silent and will not tell what I see nor their*

line 15   *words.*

The insertions in square brackets substitute missing portions of the text; those in round brackets are brief explanatory additions. (Author's note.)

PLATE XC

TOILET OF A BEAUTY
(DYNASTY XX)

Drawing on papyrus. Length 6 ¹/₄ in., width 4 in. Drovetti collection. Catalogue no. 2031

The beauty is engaged in drawing along her lips a reed held delicately in the fingers of her left hand, which has been dipped in the paint in the small jar which she is holding in her right hand, together with the handle of the mirror into which she is gazing. Her left knee steadies her left elbow, resting against it. She is intent on the most delicate of operations: that of maquillage.

Her hair falls down in numerous tiny locks to the nape of her neck. A lotus flower rests on her forehead. Her feet are bare.

The sketch of this delightful scene, in rapid strokes, is the work of an observant artist with a skilful hand!

PLATE XCI

ONERE IN THE OTHER WORLD
(DYNASTY XX)

From the papyrus " Book of the Dead " that bears his name.
Measurements: height 7 7/8 in., width 10 1/4 in. Drovetti collection. Catalogue no. 1771

The deceased, who during his life held office as priest of the Theban goddess Mut, the " lady of the heavens, " is shown, in the large vignette reproduced in the plate, engaged in two different activities of his life in the Other World. On the waters flowing through the celestial region known as the " Field of Reeds " in the religious funerary texts, the deceased, clothed in a full, pleated linen robe, his hair crowned with red vine leaves trailing down behind his shoulders, is advancing, from left to right, in the boat of the god Osiris, known as *nšm.t.*

In the top left and right corners of the scene are two big *udjat* eyes to ward off evil spirits, one of which is winged, the other raising an arm in echo of the same gesture on the part of the deceased. Below: Onere in a different linen robe, calf-length and not pleated, is goading two cows which, walking in step, are together pulling the plough for the ploughing of the " Field of Reeds. "

The magic powers attributed to Chapter VI of the " Book of the Dead, " and the services of the *shawabti*-figures (see description of Plate LXXVI), enabled the deceased Egyptians to avoid the performance of these and all other onerous or unpleasant tasks which could be imposed on them in the Other World.

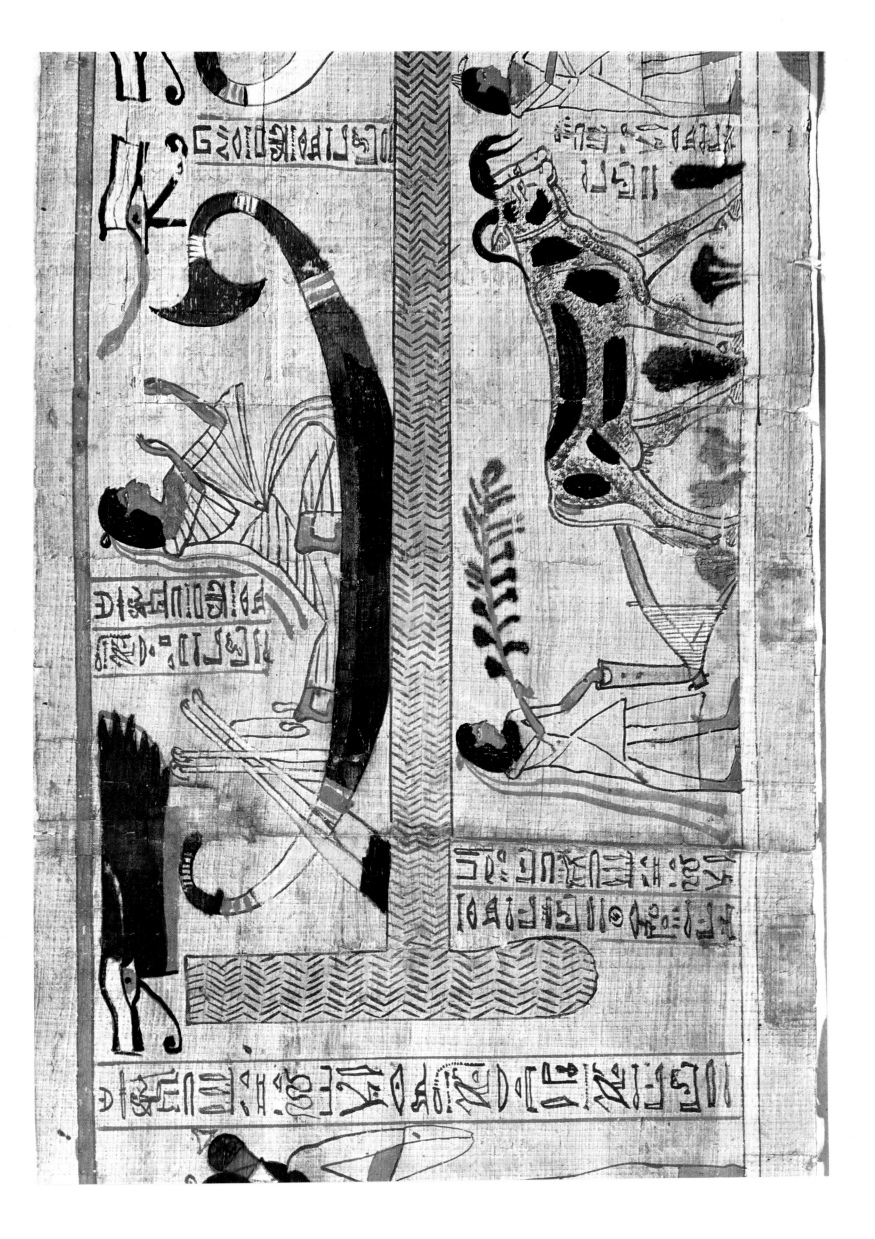

PLATE XCII

SEPULCHRAL STELA OF NES-ḤONSU-PA-KHERD
(DYNASTY XX-XXI)

Wooden stela. Height 11 ⁵/₈ in., width 6 ⁷/₈ in. Drovetti collection. Catalogue no. 1598

Above the scene which fills almost the entire surface of the stela is the pictograph of the sky, designed to fit the curve of the arch and resting on the two vertical symbols of east and west. A little below, a winged solar disk is visible between two uraei, and below it, on the left, is seated in right profile the falcon-headed god Ra-Horakhte-Atum, " lord of the two lands and of Heliopolis, " holding in his hands raised to his breast the *ḥqˀ* sceptre and a flagellum. In front of the god, to whom she proffers worship, stands the figure of the deceased, in left profile, in a long transparent white linen garment, carrying on her head the traditional pomade cone.

From the six vertical lines of text, inscribed from left to right, we learn the name of the deceased, Nes-Ḥonsu-pa-kherd (*nś-ḫnś.u-pˀ-ḫrd*) " the mistress of the house, " and the name of her mother.

This scene is followed below by a rectangular scene, smaller in scale. Beginning on the left, we recognize the conventional mode of representing the mountainous zone of the necropolis which stretched along the western bank of the Nile, opposite the ancient city of Thebes; then follows the tomb of the deceased and the funerary garden belonging to it, rich in palms and persea plants, one of which is visible on the extreme right of the scene.

LATE DYNASTIC PERIOD

Plate XCIII

THE PRIEST OF MEMPHIS, MERENPTAH
(SECOND HALF OF DYNASTY XXV)

Veined diorite statue. Height 1 ft. 3 ³/₈ in. Drovetti collection. Catalogue no. 3063

This statue, in the curious form of a block or cube in which the skilful and sensitive artist sculptured Merenptah, priest of Memphis, is so fashioned as to isolate or rather to concentrate in the face alone the most important elements of his personality. The form of the body, the garments, the details of the hair or plaits of the wig are almost eliminated, as being foreign to the planes in which the statue is modelled.

From the stylized lines of the wig, smooth in surface so as not to attract the attention of whoever examines and admires the statue, the lineaments of the face stand out in sharp contrast because of the skill with which their mobility has been shown. The face is a realistic portrait which reveals the inner workings of Merenptah's psychological make-up. The sculptor has caught and fixed the sovereign indifference of a priest no longer young, content perhaps with his self-made isolation, apart from the everyday life of his contemporaries. Given the realism with which the face is constructed, the austere gaze of the eyes is all the more disturbing in its fixity.

PLATE XCIV

STATUETTE OF AN ANONYMOUS FIGURE
(DYNASTY XXVI)

Portion of a green schist statuette.   Height 7 ¹/₄ in.   Drovetti collection.   Catalogue no. 1393

Only a small part of this statuette of a standing figure remains: the head and the right shoulder.   On the head is the wig of the period, its plaits indicated by parallel grooves, falling to cover the nape of the neck, and leaving the ears visible.   The face is in an excellent state of preservation, a fine example of Saite portraiture.   The sculptor has emphasized the eyebrows, lengthened the edges of the eyelids and cut the lips in a straight line.   The figure is beardless.

On the surviving shoulder is lightly engraved a royal cartouche containing the name of a Psammetichus, preceded by the group *s'r'* " son of the sun-god Ra, " hurriedly inscribed and terminating with the epiphoneme " living for eternity. "   In particular the graphic symbols ▢ and ∬, with which the name of Psammetichus opens, are very roughly traced.   Much more carefully inscribed, probably by another hand, are the words on the surviving portion of the rear plinth, the opening of what is commonly known as the " Saite formula, " addressed, in the interests of the individual represented in the statue, to the god of the city in which he lived.

PLATE XCV

SARCOPHAGUS OF GEMNEFHARBEK

(SAITE PERIOD)

Diorite sarcophagus, in good state of preservation. Length 7 ft. 7 ³/₈ in.; maximum width of lid 2 ft. 8 ¹/₄ in. Drovetti collection. Catalogue no. 2201

Gemnefharbek, for whom this sarcophagus was sculptured, held a number of high offices during his life-time. He was a prince, a noble, the town governor of the city in which the government resided, judge and prime minister (or vizier, to use another current translation of the title *ṭ̣ti*).

The anthropoid sarcophagus, fashioned with great art, consists of the thick and heavy lid, and the coffin. To examine first the lid: the face of the figure stands out magnificently, framed by the two thick, heavy and rigid lappets of the traditional tripartite wig, the rest of which falls behind the shoulders. The wide parallel stripes, suggestive of stylized hair, likewise contribute to accentuate the play of light and shade and the softness of the planes in the face of Gemnefharbek.

The sculptor has emphasized the slightly arched and lengthened eyebrows; he has enclosed the almond-shaped eyes between eye-lids in marked relief. The nose is rather wide at the base; well-moulded the line between the nostrils and the stylized, straight-cut lips. The ears, flattened out at the side of the face, are big; their lobes soft and fleshy. Under the rounded chin is the ritual beard of Osiris fastened to the face with a strap engraved by the sculptor along the cheeks.

The shoulders and breast of the figure are covered with a full rich necklace, made up of many chains. The image of the goddess Maat (Truth), symbolic of the high office of judge held by Gemnefharbek, which is fastened round the neck of the figure, is only faintly visible below his beard. Below the necklace a great sacred winged scarab is conspicuous, the symbol of the resurrection of all the dead identified with Osiris, according to Egyptian beliefs (see Plate XCVI). Below it are inscribed two vertical lines of text containing the " prayer for offerings ."

The coffin is distinguished by an unusual feature: the outside of the flat bottom is beautifully engraved. For this reason the coffin is exhibited face downward, so as to make clearly visible the surface which normally rests on the bare earth (see Plate XCVII).

At the top of this flat base, under the wig which 2 feet 2 inches long, is traced a rectangle 10 ¹/₄ inches by 1 feet 6 ¹/₂ inches. In this, at the sides of the large-scale *dd* column, the figure of the deceased is shown standing, paying homage, bare-headed and without wig, wearing a calf-length linen garment from his waist. Round his neck is the image of the goddess Maat. Some of the more important official posts held by Gemnefharbek are listed in horizontal and vertical lines which frame the scene at sides and top, and his name is repeated at the end of the lines. This is followed by a long inscription, from Chapter LXXII of the " Book of the Dead," on 16 horizontal lines written from right to left, 1 feet 11 ¹/₄ inches high. It is a pleasure for the eye to examine the perfectly traced hieroglyphics repeated identically in the figure with astounding precision and care. This is followed by thirteen vertical lines of hieroglyphics, 2 feet 4 ³/₈ inches high. Roughly half of these, the seven on the left reading from right to left, contain an invitation to the " Lords of Truth " to grant good burial and provisions for the deceased, whose name is repeated at the ends of the second and sixth line; the others, on the right, reading from left to right, list Gemnefharbek's *cursus honorum*, his name recurring inevitably at the ends of lines one to five. At the end of the seventh line from the left and sixth from the right are inscribed respectively the names of Gemnefharbek's father and mother.

PLATE XCVI

Detail of Plate XCV

PLATE XCVII

Detail of the outside of the bottom of the sarcophagus shown in Plate XCV

PLATE XCVII

Detail of the outside of the bottom of the sarcophagus shown in Plate XCV

PLATE XCVIII

SEPULCHRAL STELA OF PINYRIS

(LATE DYNASTIC PERIOD)

Stuccoed and painted wooden stela. Height 1 ft.: 8 in., width 1 ft. 1 3/4 in.
Drovetti collection. Catalogue no. 1569

This arch-topped stela is remarkable for the excellent state of preservation of both scenes and inscription, distributed in three unequal sections.

Conspicuous at the top is the winged solar disk of the city of Edfu, from which hang down two uraei; one of these is wearing the green royal crown of the South and one the red crown of the North. Between the uraei is the image of the *Ḫprr* scarab, sacred to the sun god. On either side reclines the god Ophois, known by the epithet of "Opener of the ways" of the south and north, at the head of the Egyptian territory, shown in the iconographic form of a jackal *couchant* with the attributes of the god.

Below, in a large rectangular scene, the deceased man (in Egyptian *pꜣ-iw-n-ḥrw*) on the left of the god is shown in profile, in a white garment with a diadem on his head. During his lifetime he held office as "the god's treasurer" and belonged to the third class or *phyle* of priests. The god Anubis, painted in black and holding in his right hand a roll of papyrus tied round with a string, introduces him to Osiris, who is seated on a throne, his hands and face painted green; he wears the emblematic *ꜣtfw* crown, a ritual beard on his chin, and holds the *ḥqꜣ* sceptre and a flagellum. Behind Osiris stand the sisters Isis and Nephthys, the falcon-headed Horus wearing a *pschent* on his head and the *wꜣs* sceptre in his left hand, and Hathor holding a papyrus sceptre, recognizable by her head-dress with the solar disk and two cow's horns.

Below this scene is inscribed a text in cursive hieroglyphics, on ten horizontal lines written from right to left. Mention should be made of the beginning, which is characteristic of the Late Dynastic Period, and which has been found also on another Turin stela (Catalogue no. 1599): "Royal decree issued by his Majesty King of South Egypt and King of North Egypt, Unnefer," and of other gods mentioned in the first and second lines.

It is interesting to note that the third and seventh lines are painted green.

The two bottom corners of the base of the stela show the damage caused by fixing it onto two wooden supports in the form of steps, which clearly had a symbolic meaning.

Plate XCIX

STELA OF A PRIEST, P꞉-Ś-ṮRF.I
(LATE DYNASTIC PERIOD)

Stuccoed and painted wooden stela.   Height 1 ft. 5 ¹/₄ in., width 11 ³/₄ in.
Drovetti collection.   Catalogue no. 1568

This fine wooden stela, arched at the top, consists of three sections; its vivid colouring still excellently preserved brings to life the scenes with which it is painted.

Conspicuous at the top is the winged solar disk of Edfu, a city known by the Greeks as Apollinopolis Megale (southern Egypt), between two uraei, distinguished by the red royal crown of the north and the white crown of the south.   Beneath is a frieze consisting of fifteen uraei with solar disks on their heads.   Below the pictograph of the sky, covered with stars, stands the deceased, paying homage on the left to the falcon-headed god Ra-Horakhte and on the right to Atum " lord of the two territories (= Egypt) and of Heliopolis. "   On two altars rest gigantic lotus flowers.

Below, in four horizontal lines of hieratic text inscribed from right to left, is the funerary prayer for offers addressed to Osiris, father-of-the-god, in the name of P꞉-ś-ṯrf.i, son of a certain P꞉-di-imn-nś-towe who held the same office in the priesthood as his son.

The solar disk at the top, and the figures of the gods Ra-Horakhte and Atum and of the deceased are all covered in gold leaf.

PLATE C

HEAD OF A PRIEST

(END OF 4th CENTURY B.C.)

Diorite head, with whitish quartz veining visible down both right and left side of the piece.
The nose and the outer part of the ears are damaged, and the chin is chipped. Height 8 $^5/_8$ in.,
width from ear to ear, 6 $^1/_4$ in. Catalogue no. 3139

The head reproduced in the plate was originally part of a statue of a priest sculptured in standing posture. The sculptor has modelled the characteristic dolichocephalic shape of the clean-shaven head, and has fashioned the face in a lengthened oval.

The rectilinear progression, without inward curvature, of the arched eyelids and the brows aids in giving the almond-shaped eyes the special emphasis which is typical of late Egyptian portraiture. Another characteristic of this late period is traceable in the moulding of the straight-cut lips, emphasized by dimples in the corners. The highly polished surface of the piece is a further indication of its date, which can definitely be ascribed to the end of the 4th century B.C.

PLATE CI

HEAD OF THE STATUE OF A KING
(PTOLEMAIC PERIOD)

Head of grey-green schist. Total height 7 $^1/_{16}$ in.; height from chin to border of " nemes" 3 $^9/_{16}$ in.;
width from ear to ear 4 $^1/_8$ in. Drovetti collection. Catalogue no. 1399

The head here reproduced was part of a less than life-size statue of a king. It is covered by a *nemes*, in the centre front of which is set a uraeus. A hole drilled in the top of the head served for the insertion of a metal decoration.

The face of the figure is markedly idealized. The shaping of the features shows no trace of the sense of volume and the firm clarity of the simple planes that is found in Egyptian statues of the best periods. The sculptor has softened the line of the brows, rounded off the outlines of the eyelids and omitted entirely to mould the lengthening of the corners of the eyes, marked in kohl.

A comparison of this Turin head with the well-known Vatican statue of Ptolemy II provides us with definite elements by which to attribute a date, so that it can be ascribed to about the beginning of the 3rd century B.C.

It is not certain which king of the Ptolemaic period is represented by the head reproduced in this plate.

PLATE CII

CRUSHING OF LILIES FOR ESSENCE
(PTOLEMAIC PERIOD)

Limestone bas-relief.   Height 1 ft. ³/₈ in., length 2 ft. 2 ³/₄ in.   Drovetti collection.   Catalogue no. 1673

In low relief on a rectangular limestone slab, once part of the wall decoration of a tomb, five young women are shown intent on crushing lily flowers for their essence, the main ingredient of the *lirinon*, the perfumed unguent which was widely used in ancient times.

Two of them, identical, stand facing each other in the centre of the composition, the same figure in the same position and with the same gestures. With sticks which they grasp in both their hands, they are twisting the ring-shaped ends of a net full of lily flowers, wringing out the essence into a large wide-brimmed, two-handled vase below (Plate CIII). On the left two other women are approaching, with flowers in their right hands and in the bags they are carrying in their left hands. In profile a fifth woman stands on the extreme right of the relief, inhaling the perfume of a flower which she is in the act of raising to her face.

The five women, all of whom are shown as being practically the same height, wear close-fitting sleeveless garments with shoulder-straps, following their movements.   Their short hair is gathered into a helmet shape. The first three women, on the left, are all wearing necklaces: the fourth has none, and in the case of the fifth the artist has merely cut the two parallel circular lines of the necklace, without adding other details.

In spite of the prevailing schematization with which the five women have been represented, and which is to be found in the slavish repetition of the identical pose, gesture and dress of the two facing figures, nevertheless the harmonious grace with which the artist has portrayed the agile movements of the women intent on their trivial feminine occupation leads us to feel that the scene has been observed and re-created with relish.

With regard to dating: this bas-relief which was first attributed to the Middle Kingdom, then to the Saite renaissance, can today be assigned to the pre-Ptolemaic or Ptolemaic periods, on account of definite Greek influence.

Plate CIII

Detail of Plate CII

PLATE CIV

BRONZE SITULA

(PTOLEMAIC PERIOD)

Cast bronze situla, well preserved. Height 8 ⁵/₈ in.; height with handle 1 ft. 1 ³/₈ in. Diameter of round brim 3 ¹/₂ in.; diameter of bowl 4 ¹/₂ in. The outer surface is divided into four sections. The first from the top contains a horizontal inscription ⁹/₁₆ in. high; the second containing two boats of the sun is 1 ¹/₈ in. high; the third containing a scene representing the deceased in the presence of gods is 3 ³/₈ in. high; the last, uninscribed, is ³/₄ in. high. Drovetti collection. Catalogue no. 3168

This fine example of a situla used in the funeral rite of the libation of life-giving water is in cast bronze with a circular brim on the rim of which are two *šn* rings; through these pass the hooked ends of a strong curved handle.

Widening toward the bottom, it ends in a semi-spherical base, *in modum papillae*, with a boss decorated with a design of lotus petals and leaves. Beginning from the top, immediately under the inscription which runs around the brim, is a section in studied relief 1 ¹/₈ inches high, are the two mythical boats of day (the *m'nḏ.t*) and of night (the *mśkt.t*). It was believed that in these boats the sun-god, Ra, made his daily voyage across the heavens, pictured as a vast area of water, and then travelled along the river of hell during the twelve hours of the night which precede his reappearance on the earth. The sun-god stands in the centre of both boats, under a canopy, holding the *w'ś* sceptre. The two boats sail from left to right. Four dog-headed figures sing praises to the first, standing upright on their hind feet; the second is drawn by four jackals, like the boat in another scene on a papyrus also housed in the Egyptian Museum, catalogued as no. 1781.

The central section of the situla is occupied by a fine relief of the deceased and seven deities. Above each figure is a tablet, standing out in relief, on which is incribed the name and the rank of each god.

The deceased can be seen standing in left profile, wearing a long garment almost down to his ankles, his arms raised in the act of homage and veneration. The tablet above his head has remained uninscribed, so that we can never know his name.

Between the deceased and the first of the gods on the left of this plate, stands a table of offerings laden with provisions. The first in the line of standing gods, all in right profile, is qualified as Amen-Ra, in the iconographic image of the ithyphallic god Min of Coptos and Panopolis, to whom the title "bull of his mother" must refer, and who is wearing the characteristic headdress of the solar disk between two long ostrich plumes. The god holds his right arm raised, a flagellum in his hand. Behind him, on the roof of a shrine, stand two *lactuca sativa longifolia* plants on either side of a lotus flower.

The three following deities all carry the *w'ś* sceptre in their left hands and the *'nh* amulet in their right. The first god is Haroeris "son of Osiris" in his iconographic falcon-headed image, with the *pschent* on his head (Plate CV). He is followed by Isis and her sister Nephthys, wearing a long garment enfolded in wide wings. Isis, the "mother of the god" Horus, is recognizable by the attributes of her head-dress: a solar disk between two cow's horns resting on the image of the sacred hawk, the symbolic attribute invariably worn by goddesses and queens. Nephthys is recognizable by the hieroglyphic symbols forming her name, resting on the image of the sacred hawk (Plate CVI). Behind these two goddesses comes the ibis-headed god Thoth, "lord" of the "city of the Eight," known by the Greeks as Hermopolis Megale (Plate CVII). Behind him are again two female figures, wearing identical long garments down to their ankles, decorated by lozenge-shaped netting and held up by shoulder straps: they carry no symbols in their hands but raise their arms in the act of homage. The better known is the first of these: *Šnt'y.t*, a cow goddess early identified with Isis, who at times is represented as weeping over the body of Osiris, and who was worshipped chiefly in the city of the Delta called by the Greeks Busiris. The latter bears the name of *'nh mrḥ.t-ś* (*'nh m rḥ.t-ś* ?). Both, we are told, were introduced to "satisfy the heart of Osiris, their lord".

Plate CV

A successive view of the situla in Plate CIV

Plate CV

A successive view of the situla in Plate CIV

PLATE CVI

A successive view of the situla in Plate CIV

PLATE CVI

PLATE CVII

A successive view of the situla in Plate CIV

PLATE CVII

PLATE CVIII

LID OF WOODEN COFFIN OF DJED-THOTH-EF-'ONCH

(4th CENTURY B.C.)

Sycamore wood lid. Irregular fragment. Height 2 ft. 3 ¹/₂ in., width about 1 ft. 1 in.
Drovetti collection. Catalogue no. 2241

The plate reproduces the lower central portion of the lid of a wooden sarcophagus, which has been sawn off without the slightest attention being paid to the fine example of hieroglyphics in coloured enamels with which it is ornamented.

The coffin was made for Djed-Thoth-ef-'onch (*ḏd-ḏḥuti-i[u]-f-'nḫ*), named after one of his ancestors. He lived in Hermopolis Megale during the 4th century B.C., dying there at no great age and without descendants. A better-known member of his family was his younger brother Petosiris, who enjoyed considerable fame in the same city, living many years and holding high office, serving as the high priest of the local god, Thoth. The French archaeologist Gustave Lefebvre in 1920 brought to light his monumental tomb in Tuna el-Gebel, roughly ten miles to the north of Hermopolis Megale.

The five longitudinal lines of inscription, slightly damaged in that some of the hieroglyphic symbols have fallen out, must have contained, in the first line on the right and most of the second line, the name of the deceased, that of his parents and his *cursus honorum*; the rest of the text, from the remaining portion of the second line on, contained Chapter LXXII of the "Book of the Dead," in the version current in the Late Dynastic Period. Through the reprehensible carelessness of whoever sawed off the fragment, the first part of every line is missing; the lost text has been calculated as about half the length of the surviving portion.

Even in the state to which it has been reduced, this fragment called forth expressions of enthusiastic admiration from Champollion, who examined it at length on the occasion of his first stay in Turin. A detailed examination shows that each of the single hieroglyphic symbols has been fashioned with the maximum figurative precision and attention to minutiae, and painted in enamels of one or more colours. The monochrome symbols most frequently repeated are the signs ⌡ = *b*; ✍ = *f*; ▭ = *m*; ∿ = *n*; ⚄ = *ḥ*; △ = *t*; ⚬ = *wn*, all in green, and the definite articles 𓏏; 𓏤; ▱, in coral pink. Among the polychrome symbols, so skilfully assembled that they deserve to be examined and admired one by one, are the signs 𓏲 = '; 𓏱 = *w*; ■ = *p*; ◉ = *ḫ*; the eye '⌲ (verb *to do*); the basket ⌣ = *nb* (Plate CIX).

These symbols were inlaid in hollows prepared for them, cut in the wooden lid, the exact shape and size having been precisely calculated.

Also Petosiris, the younger brother of the deceased, had the lid of one of his wooden coffins, now housed in the Cairo Museum, inlaid in the same way with Chapter LXXII of the "Book of the Dead" in enamelled hieroglyphics.

This type of ornament dates back in Egypt to the Old Kingdom, as is shown by fragments of wooden vases with enamelled incrustations found in the area of the temple in Abusir, dating from the reign of King Neferirkara; the fragment of an ivory casket found at Lisht with hieroglyphs modelled in carnelian, bearing the name of king Acthoes, dates back to the First Intermediate Period; the limestone fragments of sarcophagi decorated with enamels which were purchased some years ago by the Louvre Museum are of a later period, pertaining to the 26th dynasty.

Plate CIX

Detail of Plate CVIII

PLATE CX

A QUEEN

(PTOLEMAIC PERIOD)

Black granite fragment. The nose damaged and the face slightly chipped. The " modius " on the head has been lost.
Total height 1 ft. 9 ¹/₄ in.; height of face from chin to wig 4 ¹/₈ in.; width from ear to ear 5 ¹/₂ in.
Catalogue no. 1385

This fragment, broken off obliquely a little below the breasts, is part of a statue of a queen of the Ptolemies who cannot be identified with certainty. She is sculptured standing with her arms down by her sides.

The face of the young woman is framed by two full, stylized braids which fall over her shoulders to the top of her breasts in the customary three divisions, the remainder falling in tiny parallel plaits behind her shoulders, brushing the top of the square-cut rear plinth.

On her hair the sculptor has modelled the image of the sacred hawk, the invariable symbol of Egyptian goddesses and queens, adopted also by the female figures of the Ptolemies. The long open wings of the bird of prey fall down in stylized lines behind the ears, while the tail feathers and the ends of the claws, gripping two *šn* rings, are visible at the back of the queen's head. The top of the head must originally have carried the attribute of a circular *modius*, of which the perimeter of the base is still visible. Over the brow of the queen are three uraei, an unusual number, which are first documented as occurring in the colossal statuary group of Queen Tiy and her husband Amenhotep III of the 18th dynasty, from Medinet Habu. Professor H. Wolfgang Müller has advanced the theory that the central uraeus is an assimilation of the hawk's head to the form of the uraei on either side.

The face of the queen shows traces of Greek influence in new characteristics that contrast with the formal Egyptian elements of the piece such as the rear plinth, the three divisions of the hair, etc. The soft lips are moulded with a natural movement, not with Egyptian stylization, nor is their cut stylized, and they are set between full curved cheeks and a rounded chin. The eyes are slightly sunken between the cheek-bones and the strongly arched eyebrows, and are bordered with lightly-marked lids.

The queen is not nude but is wearing a thin tunic of which the neckline is visible above her breasts.

PLATE CXI

Side view of the statuary fragment in Plate CX

PLATE CXII

MALE HEAD

(Ist CENTURY B.C.)

Black granite head. Nose, ears and upper lip damaged; lesser chips on left eyebrow and chin. Total height,
including neck 7 ¹/₂ in.; height from brow to chin 5 ¹¹/₁₆ in.; width from ear to ear 5 ¹¹/₁₆ in.
Obtained by exchange from the Kircherian Museum in Rome.

The head, detached from a lost statue, less than life-size, is that of a
man in his prime. At the back may be seen a hole in the nape of the neck
cut with a view either to re-using the head at a later date, or to fit it to
some special support.

The hair is represented in markedly flat curls, shorter over the brows
and longer at the temples, without any detailed modelling. At the back
these curls cover the nape of the neck. The ears are small, and are placed
in a natural position at the side of the head. The forehead is smooth. The
face is slightly lengthened in form. Under the line of the eyebrows the
sculptor has set the eyes rather obliquely, bordered by corded lashes. The
nose must have been small, with narrow nostrils. The ridge of the cheek-
bones on the smooth, thin, hairless cheeks is only slightly visible, while the
wrinkles running from nose to mouth are cut in a decisive stylized line.
The lips, although prominent, are not full; the mouth is small, cut in an
uncompromising straight line, and with dimples at the corners. The chin
is small and rounded.

The head cannot be connected with others modelled in the Late Dynastic
Period, in the peculiar taste of portrait sculpture of the time: sculpture
in the latter style blended, more or less consciously and successfully,
the national tradition with innovations borrowed from or modelled on
the techniques and tendencies of the art of the alien rulers, the Greeks.
It is, instead, a good example of the current of Egyptian sculpture which,
eliminating any tendency to idealize the human figure, aimed at reproducing
the natural and individual characteristics of the subject, using a minimum
of means of expression.

Examples like this head are few and far between in Egyptian collections
today: for this reason it is difficult to date the piece with any accuracy.
Taking into account the modelling of the hair, which is no longer Egyptian
in form but has flattened curls (a style which came into existence about
the second half of the second century B.C.), and noting also a preference for
greater simplicity in the modelling of the features which likewise became
current at the same period, this head can be dated in the first century B.C.,
or more precisely in the second half of the first century.

PLATE CXIII

RELIEF SHOWING WILD BEASTS AND THE PLANT OF LIFE
(COPTIC, 6th-7th CENTURY A.D.)

Limestone relief. Height 1 ft. 5 ³/₈ in., width 2 ft. 3 ¹/₂ in.
Purchased by Ernesto Schiaparelli in Egypt. Catalogue supplement no. 1339

In high relief two felines, the male on the left, the female on the right, are standing at either side of a big two-handled vase with a circular brim on a funnel-shaped neck, the bowl of which stands high behind luxuriant leaves, opening out like a fan.

The scene represented is slightly damaged: the beast on the left has lost its right front paw, the claws of which are visible on one of the leaves which cover the bowl of the vase; the other beast has lost its left front paw, the claws of which are recognizable on a leaf at the bottom right, while the hind paws are also damaged. The pupils of the creatures' eyes are conspicuous, the holes having been drilled.

The pair are engaged in defending the sacred plant which springs from the mouth of the vase. Their muzzles are clearly turned outward in open threat, detached from the ground plane of the relief.

Behind the beast, in bas-relief, stands a tree with three leafy branches.

The subject is a repetition of an ancient motif, of oriental origin, from Mesopotamia. It is a subject rarely treated in Coptic sculpture and for this reason it has been thought fitting to take this opportunity of bringing it to the knowledge of students of Coptic art.

The workmanship is commonplace, so that even the threat of the snapping jaws of the roaring beasts seems conventional and frigid (Plate CXIV).

Plate CXIV

Detail of Plate CXIII

SELECTED BIBLIOGRAPHY

BAROCELLI, P., *Il viaggio del dott. Vitaliano Donati in Oriente (1759-62) in relazione colle prime origini del Museo Egiziano di Torino*, in "Atti R. Accad. delle Scienze," Turin, vol. XLVII, 1912.

ČERNÝ, J., *Egyptian Stelae in the Bankes Collection*, Oxford, 1958.

CHAMPOLLION le Jeune, *Lettres à M. le Duc de Blacas d'Aulps relatives au Musée Royale de Turin*, Paris, 1824, 1826.

FARINA, G., *Il papiro dei Re restaurato*, Rome, 1938.

GARDINER, A. H., *The Royal Canon of Turin*, Oxford, 1959.

GARDINER, A. H., *Egypt of the Pharaohs*, Oxford, 1961.

GAZZERA, C., *Descrizione dei Monumenti Egizi del R. Museo a Torino contenenti leggende reali*, Turin-Naples, 1824.

GAZZERA, C., *Applicazione delle dottrine del Sig. Champollion Minore ad alcuni monumenti geroglifici del R. Museo Egizio*, in "Mem. Accad. delle Scienze," Turin, vol. XXIX (1825), p. 83 ff.

LANZONE, R. V., *Dizionario di Mitologia Egizia*, Turin, 1881-85.

MARRO, G., *La personalità di Bernardino Drovetti studiata nel suo archivio inedito*, in "Mem. Accad. delle Scienze," Turin, series II, vol. 71, part II, cl. Scienze Mor. St. Filol., 1951.

ORCUTI, P.-C., *Catalogo illustrato dei Monumenti Egizi del R. Museo di Torino*, vols. I-II, Turin, 1852, 1855.

ROSSI, FR., *I Monumenti Egizi del Museo di Antichità di Torino*, Turin, 1884.

ROSSI, FR., FABRETTI, A., LANZONE, R. V., *Regio Museo di Torino. Antichità Egizie*, vols. I-II, Rome, 1881, 1888.

SCAMUZZI, E., *La Mensa Isiaca*, Rome, 1939.

SCHIAPARELLI, E., *Relazione sui lavori della Missione Archeologica Italiana in Egitto*. Vol. I, *Esplorazione della "Valle delle Regine" nella necropóli di Tebe*, Turin, 1924; Vol. II, *La tomba intatta dell'architetto Cha nella necropoli di Tebe*, Turin, 1927.

VANDIER, J., *Manuel d'Archéologie Égyptienne*. Vol. III: *Les grandes époques. La Statuaire*, Paris, 1958.

PRINTED BY POLIGRAFICHE RIUNITE
FRATELLI POZZO - SALVATI - GROS MONTI & C. - S. p. A.
TURIN, 1965